World of Art

Sir Nikolaus Pevsner, born in Germany in 1902, was educated at the universities of Leipzig, Munich, Berlin and Frankfurt, and took his PhD in the History of Art and Architecture in 1924. He was Assistant Keeper at the Dresden Gallery, 1924–28, and Lecturer in the History of Art and Architecture at Göttingen University, 1929–33. Later he left Germany to live in Britain, where he was Slade Professor of Fine Art, University of Cambridge, 1949–55, and Fellow of St John's College, 1950–55. He was the first Professor of the History of Art Department at Birkbeck College, University of London, retiring in 1969. He is probably best known for *The Buildings of England*, completed in more than 50 volumes shortly before his death, and for his *Outline of European Architecture*, which has remained a standard work for over forty years. Other books include *Pioneers of Modern Design*, *The English-ness of English Art*, *Studies in Art, Architecture and Design* (collected essays from all stages of his career) and *A History of Building Types*. He died in 1983.

Kenneth Frampton CBE was born in 1930 and trained as an architect at the Architectural Association School of Architecture, London. He has taught at a number of leading institutions in the field, including the Royal College of Art in London, the ETH in Zürich, the Berlage Institute in Amsterdam, EPFL in Lausanne and the Accademia di Architettura in Mendrisio. From 1972 to 2019 he served as Ware Professor of Architecture at the Graduate School of Architecture, Planning and Preservation, Columbia University, New York. He is the author of numerous essays on modern and contemporary architecture, has served on many international juries for architectural awards and building commissions, and is a member of the American Academy of Arts and Letters. In 2018 he was awarded the Golden Lion of the Venice Biennale. His publications include *Studies in Tectonic Culture* (1992), *Labour, Work and Architecture* (2005), *American Masterworks* (2008), *Kengo Kuma: Complete Works* (2012) and *A Genealogy of Modern Architecture* (2013).

T0285216

1 Palm House, Kew Gardens, 1848

World of Art

The Sources of Modern Architecture and Design
Nikolaus Pevsner

Foreword by Kenneth Frampton

New edition

First published in 1968 in the United Kingdom
by Thames & Hudson Ltd, 181A High Holborn,
London WC1V 7QX

www.thamesandhudson.com

First published in 1968 in the United States of
America by Thames & Hudson Inc., 500 Fifth Avenue,
New York, New York 10110

www.thamesandhudsonusa.com

Reprinted 1989

This new edition published in 2024

The Sources of Modern Architecture and Design © 1968 and
2024 Thames & Hudson Ltd, London

Text by Nikolaus Pevsner © 1968 Verlag Georg D. W. Callwey

Foreword © 2024 Kenneth Frampton

Art direction and series design by Kummer and Herrman
Layout by Adam Hay Studio

British Library Cataloguing-in-Publication Data
A catalogue record for this book is available from
the British Library

Library of Congress Control Number 2023950413

ISBN 978-0-500-29769-8

Printed and bound in China by Asia Pacific Offset Ltd

MIX
Paper from
responsible sources
FSC® C136333
FSC
www.fsc.org

Contents

6   Foreword by Kenneth Frampton

9   Introduction

Chapter 1
11   **A Style for the Age**

Chapter 2
45   **Art Nouveau**

Chapter 3
117   **New Impetus from England**

Chapter 4
149   **Art and Industry**

Chapter 5
179   **Towards the International Style**

202   Notes on the Text
203   Biographical Notes
210   Sources of Illustrations
213   Select Bibliography
214   Index

Foreword
Kenneth Frampton

First researched by Nikolaus Pevsner in the early 1930s as a
young professor at Göttingen University, this study – which
focuses on the implicit symbiotic relationship between
decorative art and architecture, particularly during the last
half of the nineteenth century and the first decade of the
twentieth – is related to the material he covered in his *Pioneers
of the Modern Movement: From William Morris to Walter Gropius*,
published in 1936, just three years after his arrival in Britain.

Thirty-two years later came *The Sources of Modern
Architecture and Design*, which takes as its subject the craft
origins of the modern movement rather than the 'pioneers', and
traces the alleged affinity between the nostalgic reformism of
William Morris's Arts and Crafts Red House in Bexleyheath,
Kent (1859), designed by Philip Webb, and Walter Gropius and
Adolf Meyer's ferrovitreous Fagus Factory, Lower Saxony (1913),
and their equally functionalist model factory built for the
Deutscher Werkbund exhibition in Cologne in 1914.

Influenced, as he himself admitted, by the fashionable Art
Nouveau revival that swept across Europe in the 1960s, Pevsner
devotes the largest chapter of his *Sources* to this style. The name
was coined by the art dealer Samuel Siegfried Bing to refer
to the decorative art objects sold in his Parisian gallery, also
called L'Art Nouveau, which featured interior decoration by the
Belgian architect Henry van de Velde (1895–6), among others.
Pevsner would become one of the first to point out that Van
de Velde's organic 'form-force' aesthetics, arising theoretically
out of the gesture of the craftsman shaping an object, would
eventually acquire the tautness of his so-called 'yachting' style

in furniture, which attained its most monumental expression in the desk he designed for the German art critic Julius Meier-Graefe in 1897. By virtue of his so-called 'Kunstseminar', consisting of 'hands-on' instruction, organized under the patronage of the Grand Duke of Saxe-Weimar in order to improve the skill and taste of local craftsmen, Van de Velde would lay the groundwork for Walter Gropius's Bauhaus, established in Weimar in 1919 in the aftermath of the first industrialized war.

Pevsner is at pains to credit the British architect Arthur Heygate Mackmurdo with the earliest excursus into the exotic 'whiplash' aesthetic of Art Nouveau, which somewhat incongruously first appears on the cover of Mackmurdo's book on Wren's City churches of 1883 and in the carved back of a chair that he designed the same year. As Pevsner makes clear, it is Mackmurdo's influence on Charles F. Annesley Voysey and Charles Rennie Mackintosh that would take the new style into Austria and Germany, where it soon became known as the 'Jugendstil'. The other strand entered Belgium via Morris's protégé Walter Crane and the Belgian furniture designer Gustave Serrurier-Bovy, who had worked in Britain and whose pieces would exercise an influence on Van de Velde. Needless to say, Pevsner continues to trace this quite literal flowering of environmental culture in the work of Victor Horta in Brussels, Hector Guimard in Paris and Antoni Gaudí in Barcelona, seen as manifestations of the same transcontinental impulse.

Although Pevsner does not acknowledge the debt for our knowledge of the dematerialized ferrovitreous form of nineteenth-century engineering to Sigfried Giedion's *Bauen in Frankreich* (1928) and the pioneering essays of P. Morton Shand that appeared regularly in the *Architectural Review* between 1920 and 1925, he would nonetheless acknowledge not only the way in which the rich legacy of Art Nouveau would be totally eclipsed by the First World War, but also the modernizing, egalitarian impulse that was emanating from the American Midwest: the initial technical and cultural rationalization of high-rise form that began with the architect Louis Sullivan, and the new cantilevered domestic architecture of his protégé, Frank Lloyd Wright, which opened up the interior of the house to the benevolence of nature surrounding it on all sides. This much Pevsner acknowledges by devoting a whole spread to Wright's Martin House, Buffalo, of 1903–5. It is odd, given how he recognizes the importance of Wright's Wasmuth portfolio (first published in Berlin, 1910), that Pevsner would not mention, nor illustrate, Gropius and Meyer's 1914 model factory, which comprised an office building plus a ferrovitreous shed – an omission made all the more curious by the fact that the thin, oversailing roofs of the office building were so evidently Wrightian.

Despite the graceful style, measured erudition and perceptive judgment, there is a dichotomy in Pevsner's world-view that is never fully articulated, for while he is appreciative of the Deutscher Werkbund's drive towards a normative industrial culture, accessible to society as a whole, he nonetheless remains as nostalgic as William Morris for that lost spiritual unity that was once as evident in painting as it was in architecture and design. Aside from prevailing fashion at the time of writing, this may well account for Pevsner's somewhat atypical preoccupation with art nouveau and for his post-facto approval of Gropius's decision in 1919 to incorporate painters into the faculty of the Bauhaus. Conversely, it also explains Pevsner's disapproval of Gropius's subsequent embrace of industrialized building and his comparable distaste for the reductive anti-Jugendstil, abstract manner of Adolf Loos's Steiner Villa in Vienna (1910). In the face of this schism, it is perhaps no accident that he should conclude his *Sources*, somewhat arbitrarily, with the irregular picturesque of the British garden city movement, which – surprisingly enough – at the beginning of the last century was as much a preoccupation with the leading architects of the Werkbund as their parallel concern with the creation of an industrial civilization.

Introduction

Where lie the sources of the twentieth century? Sources bespeak a stream, then a river, and finally, in our particular case, the ocean of the International Style of the 1930s. Do Prometheus and the unknown inventor of the wheel stand by the source as the *genii fontis*? No; because there are breaks, and our civilization is not connected with that distant past by a continuous flow. But even if we admit that civilizations 'rise and fall, crumble, are extended, Are renewed, destroyed', even if we keep within Western civilization, are the sources of the twentieth century then the invention of clocks with wheels and weights and of printing with movable type? They are; for without printing and clocking-in there could be no twentieth century. Mass communication and mass production are among the things distinguishing ours from all preceding centuries. However, it is only the quantitative exploitation which belongs exclusively to us, not the invention itself. And that is indeed a phenomenon to rank high in force among the sources of the twentieth century and therefore of modern art.

The twentieth century is the century of the masses: mass education, mass entertainment, mass transport, universities with twenty thousand students, comprehensive schools for two thousand children, hospitals with two thousand beds, stadia with a hundred thousand seats. That is one aspect; the other is speed of locomotion, every citizen being an express-train driver on his own, and some pilots travelling faster than sound. Both are only expressions of the technological fanaticism of the age, and technology is only an application of science.

Science, technology, mass locomotion, mass production and consumption, mass communication – in the field of the visual arts which is our field in this book, that means the predominance of architecture and design over the *beaux-arts*, it means the predominance of the city over the small town and the country, and it means the concentration on architecture and design for the masses and on what new materials and new techniques can do for them.

If this is accepted as a diagram of the twentieth century, so far as we can observe and analyse it, where do its sources lie then? We can now endeavour to list and consider them in their order of time.

Chapter 1
A Style for the Age

Architecture and design for the masses must be functional, in the sense that they must be acceptable to all and that their well-functioning is the primary necessity. A chair can be uncomfortable and a work of art, but only the occasional connoisseur can be expected to prefer its aesthetic to its utilitarian qualities. The plea for functionalism is the first of our sources. Augustus Welby Northmore Pugin, born in 1812, the English son of a French father, wrote on the first page of his most important book: 'There should be no features about a building which are not necessary for convenience, construction, or propriety... The smallest detail should ... serve a purpose, and construction itself should vary with the material employed.'[1] That was written in 1841, but it was not new then. It is the direct continuation of the principle of French seventeenth and eighteenth century rationalism. Architecture, writes Batteaux,[2] 'is not a spectacle ... but a service', and 'security, fitness, convenience, propriety' are all familiar from Cordemoy to Boffrand and the younger Blondel. To quote two less familiar passages, neither French: Hogarth called the first chapter of his *Analysis of Beauty*, 'Of Fitness', starting thus: 'Fitness of the parts to the design for which every individual thing is form'd ... is of the greatest consequence to the beauty of the whole... In ship-building the dimensions of every part are confin'd and regulated by fitness for sailing. When a vessel sails well, the sailors call her a beauty; the two ideas have such a connection.'[3] And the Abbate Lodoli, not uninfluenced perhaps by Hogarth, referred in his stimulating conversations to the Venetian gondola as a piece of functional design, and stipulated that nothing ought to appear in a building which is not 'truly fulfilling its function' or: 'has not its own proper function' and is not 'an integral part of the fabric' and designed in a logical relation to the 'nature of the material'.[4]

The fact that Pugin, who came first in this string of quotations, called the book which he started with this clarion call *The True Principles of Pointed or Christian Architecture*, the fact that his principal purpose was not a plea for functionalism but for the Gothic Revival as the expression of a Catholic Revival, even the fact that he argued extremely intelligently the functional aspect of the Gothic style, of buttresses, of rib-vaults and so on, all these facts do not concern us at present. He was read by the Gothicists, but he was also read by the Functionalists. For such existed among the mid-nineteenth century writers and thinkers. Gottfried Semper in Germany, with his explanation of the applied or decorative arts as conditioned by materials and techniques, was one of them. He had lived in London as a refugee in the years 1851–5, and must have been in contact with the small group of architects, artists and administrators responsible for the preparation, the success and the ruthless criticism of the Great Exhibition of 1851: Henry Cole in the first place, Owen Jones, Matthew Digby Wyatt and Richard Redgrave in the second.

These men, even before the exhibition, had issued a small journal called the *Journal of Design and Manufactures* and in this had applied the principles of Pugin, as Semper was going to do later, to matters of craft and industrial art. Pugin had objected to carpets where one walks 'upon highly relieved foliage',[5] the *Journal* now insisted that carpets should keep to 'a level or low plane',[6] that wallpapers should convey 'the proper impression of flatness'[7] and in a more general way, that 'the first consideration of the designer should be perfect adaptation to intended use'[8] and that every object 'to afford perfect pleasure must be fit for the purpose and true in its construction'.[9]

No wonder that these men, when the Crystal Palace had gone up and been filled with the proudest products of all nations, were appalled at the standard of taste displayed. 'The absence of any fixed principle in ornamental design is most apparent,' they wrote, and 'the taste of the producers is uneducated'.[10] No wonder either that they admired the Crystal Palace itself.

2   The Crystal Palace is the mid-nineteenth century touchstone, if one wishes to discover what belongs wholly to the nineteenth century and what points forward into the twentieth. The Crystal Palace was entirely of iron and glass, it was designed by a non-architect, and it was designed for industrial quantity production of its parts. It is a source in one sense, but it also had its sources, and they take us back once again to the eighteenth century. The use of iron in architecture starts

2 The Crystal Palace, built for the Great Exhibition of 1851 and re-erected at Sydenham in 1853. Joseph Paxton's building, which was entirely prefabricated, marked the first major escape from historical styles in architecture

in France in the 1780s with Soufflot and Victor Louis, who were especially concerned with making theatres fireproof, and in England in the 1790s with manufacturers who, acting as their own designers, attempted to make their factories fireproof. In both cases the iron was an expedient of high utilitarian but of no aesthetic significance. It came into the open, as it were, playfully and only internally, in some romantic buildings such as Nash's Royal Pavilion at Brighton in 1815–20, and seriously and externally in the great bridges of the same years. The earliest iron bridge was in fact designed as early as 1777 – the Coalbrookdale Bridge in England. It has a span of 30 metres (100 ft). It was at once surpassed by the bridge at Sunderland which in 1793–6 spanned 62 metres (206 ft), and this by James Finley's Schuylkill Bridge of 1809, with 93 metres (306 ft). The two English bridges had been iron arches, the Schuylkill Bridge was a suspension bridge, and the suspension principle gave us the finest of the early nineteenth-century bridges such as Thomas Telford's Menai Bridge of 1818–26 with a main span of 176 metres (579 ft).

3 LEFT Coalbrookdale Bridge, Shropshire, 1777–81, the first iron bridge in the world. Its builder, the ironmaster Abraham Darby, was assisted by a minor architect, T. F. Pritchard. The bridge crosses the Severn with a span of one hundred feet
4 OPPOSITE The Menai Suspension Bridge, linking North Wales with the Isle of Anglesey, was built by Thomas Telford between 1818 and 1826 as part of the Holyhead to Chester Road. Telford, the greatest road and canal engineer of the early nineteenth century, had earlier designed a vast single-span iron bridge of unprecedented boldness (never built) to replace London Bridge

Some architects later in the nineteenth century – Matthew Digby Wyatt among them – were ready to count them among the finest structures of the century. But they were not the work of architects. The architects, as we have seen, had been ready to use iron in a minor way, where necessity arose, but otherwise at best they only played with it. Now this is what Wyatt wrote in 1850–1, apropos the bridges, these 'wonders of the world': 'From such beginnings what glories may be in reserve ... we may trust ourselves to dream, but we dare not predict.'[11] This was the year of the Crystal Palace. Pugin called it the 'glass monster',[12] Ruskin a 'cucumber frame',[13] but Wyatt wrote that the building was likely to accelerate the 'consummation devoutly to be wished' and that 'the novelty of its form and details ... will exercise a powerful influence upon national taste'.[14] A little later he even foretold from the union of iron and glass 'a new era in architecture'.[15] This was still in 1851.

5 OPPOSITE Part of the iron-galleried interior of the Coal Exchange in London, by J. B. Bunning (1846–9). Its demolition in 1962 was one of London's most serious and futile recent losses

6 ABOVE The Bibliothèque Ste-Geneviève in Paris, by Henri Labrouste (1843–50), an iron-frame structure frankly revealed as such. At this date iron-framing was normally given a stone or plaster disguise

But by then, a few of the most adventurous architects of repute had begun to take notice of iron, and Labrouste's Bibliothèque Ste-Geneviève in Paris of 1843–50 and Bunning's Coal Exchange in London of 1846–9 remain the earliest buildings whose aesthetic character is determined by iron. Labrouste's has the greater elegance and ornamental restraint, as Labrouste was indeed doubtless the better architect of the two. That comes out even more clearly in the exteriors: Bunning's of an unprincipled jollity which was accepted at the time in England as belonging to the Free or Mixed Renaissance; Labrouste's also of the Renaissance and also a free Renaissance, but treated nobly, with discipline and economy of decoration. And both architects hid their display of iron behind solid stone.

5, 6

A Style for the Age

Wyatt appreciated Bunning, a greater man appreciated Labrouste and was guided by him: Emanuel Viollet-le-Duc (1814–79). When Labrouste stopped teaching, his pupils induced Viollet-le-Duc to take over, and he taught for a short time. In connection with this he began to deliver his *Entretiens* in 1858, published the first volume in 1863 and the more important second in 1872. His approach to architecture is the functionalist's. He demands the 'alliance of form with need' and with 'the means of construction'.[16] He demands truth: that 'stone should appear as stone, iron as iron and wood as wood',[17] that no 'monumental appearances should conceal bourgeois habits'.[18] And consequently he insists on the necessity of a style for the nineteenth century. Today, he says, 'we possess immense resources provided by industry and ease of transportation.'[19] Architecture belongs 'almost as much to science as to art'.[20] Architects must cease to be interested only in whether their façades are to be Roman, Gothic or Renaissance. From that attitude 'nothing new or living can come'.[21] When engineers invented the locomotive 'it did not occur to them to imitate the harness of a stage coach'.[22] If architects want to prevent their profession from becoming obsolete they must become 'skilful constructors, ready to take advantage of all the resources furnished by our society'.[23] And so he arrives at iron, proposes iron even for ribs in vaults (as Boileau had already shown it in Paris churches) and even for externally visible framing.

Bold words indeed, but what were the deeds? Viollet-le-Duc was the great restorer of French cathedrals, the great scholar of Gothic architecture – though admittedly with a keen sense of structure. Like Pugin before him, he did not practise what he preached. His opposite number in England was Sir George Gilbert Scott, also a self-confident restorer, also a scholar of Gothic architecture of no mean achievement, who could write: 'An iron arched bridge may always be made beautiful, and it would be difficult to make a suspension bridge anything else' and 'It is self-evident that ... modern metallic construction opens out a perfectly new field for architectural development.'[24]

But it was not his field, as it was not Viollet-le-Duc's. When he was asked to design a hotel in connection with the new St Pancras Station in London, he provided a towering Gothic pile hiding entirely the magnificent metallic construction which the engineer William H. Barlow had erected behind it as a train-shed and which, with its span of 74 metres (243 ft), was the largest span ever, until then, achieved by man. It remained the largest in Europe for twenty-five years, until it was finally vastly surpassed by Dutert and Contamin's splendid *Halle des Machines* at the Paris Exhibition of 1889, with its 110 metre (362 ft) span.

7 W. H. Barlow's train-shed of St Pancras Station, London, of 1864: a tremendous feat of engineering with its pointed arch spanning 243 feet

But while iron and glass, and the new aesthetic vocabulary which its extensive use entailed, went on in exhibition buildings and train-sheds and also in factories and office buildings, where much light and a cellular structure were demanded, the architect continued to keep away from the new materials and to be satisfied with the trappings of Gothic, Renaissance and – more and more – Baroque. Neither the aesthetic possibilities of defeating the limitation of past styles by means of the new possibilities of skeletal construction nor the social possibilities of mass-produced parts were taken seriously by the profession.

The great impetus in the fields of aesthetic and social renewal came from England and centres in the larger-than-life figure of William Morris, poet, pamphleteer, reformer, designer – trained a little at university, a little in architecture, a little in painting – and ending by being a manufacturer and shopkeeper, though a very special one. Morris's firm was started in 1861, in collaboration with his close friends, the architect Philip Webb and the painters Ford Madox Brown, Rossetti and Burne-Jones.

8 The *Hall des Machines*, built for the Paris Exhibition of 1889. It was primarily the work of engineers, led by V. Contamin, though assisted in the details by the architect Dutert – a pattern that was to become characteristic in the future

Morris's theories, as he lived them from when he was twenty-five and as he expounded them in impetuous lectures from when he was over forty, are familiar. They derive from Ruskin who had hated the Crystal Palace, had gone out of his way to say that a railway station could never be architecture and denied with frantic fanaticism the necessity for his age to search for a style of its own: 'A day never passes without our ... architects being called upon to be original and to invent a new style... We want no new style of architecture... It does not matter one marble splinter whether we have an old or new architecture... The forms of architecture already known to us are good enough for us, and far better than any of us'.[25] Morris was wiser. He refuted the current historicism, the 'masquerading in other people's cast-off clothes',[26] but he too recommended architects to 'study the ancient work directly and to learn to understand it'.[27] He was not a revolutionary; he loved the Middle Ages and loved nature and the open country, and he hated the big cities. His hatred was visual at first, but turned social almost at once. London to him was not only 'a whole county covered with hideous hovels',[28] but also a 'beastly congregation of smokedried swindlers and their slaves'.[29] The Middle Ages were not only pleasing to his eyes, they were also – as they had been to Ruskin – right in their social structure, or what he believed to have been their social structure. In the Middle Ages, he said, art was not 'divided among great men, lesser men, and little men',[30] artists were not, as they are now, 'highly cultivated men whose education enables them, in the contemplation of the past glories of the world, to shut out from their view the everyday squalors that most of men live in'.[31] Artists were plain workmen, 'common fellows' who worked away 'on the anvil' or 'about the oak beam' with 'many a grin of pleasure'.[32] The things which are museum pieces now 'were common things in their own day'.[33] And the reason why that was so, is that in the Middle Ages 'daily labour was sweetened by the daily creation of Art'.[34] And so Morris arrived at his definition of art as 'the expression by man of his pleasure in labour'.[35] He arrived at the demand that art should become this again: 'a happiness for the maker and the user.' For while the average man can have no interest in the self-conscious isolated artist, he can enjoy what the craftsman does for him. So art should be not only 'by the people' but also 'for the people'.[36] 'I do not want art for a few, any more than I want education for a few, or freedom for a few.'[37]

It is a strange system of theory to be guided by for a man in the mid-nineteenth century. It can only be understood as a demonstration of opposition to the standard and the taste of design as it was exhibited at the Great Exhibition of London in 1851, Paris in 1855, London again in 1862 and Paris again in 1867.

Looking at the goods, especially the domestic goods, illustrated in the catalogues of these exhibitions, one can understand Morris's outbursts. In the Middle Ages 'everything which was made by man's hand was more or less beautiful,' today 'almost all wares that are made by civilized man are shabbily and pretentiously ugly.'[38] What is offered and sold is 'hurtful to the buyer, more hurtful to the seller, if he only knew'.[39] Our houses are filled with 'tons upon tons of unutterable rubbish', and the only acceptable things are usually in the kitchen.[40] The reason is that they alone are honest and simple, and 'the two virtues most needed in modern life (are) honesty and simplicity'.[41] Morris maintained that a bonfire ought to have been made of nine-tenths of all that was in wealthy people's houses.[42]

Morris in his own day was no doubt right in blaming industry. 'As a condition of life, production by machinery is altogether an evil.'[43] But if you refuse to accept the machine, you cannot produce cheaply. What Morris's firm made was bound to be expensive, and could not be 'for the people'. Nor was it strictly speaking 'by the people'; for Morris and his friends designed their chintzes and wallpapers, their furniture and stained glass, and while it was made, admittedly, by hand (though not always), it was not really creative craft. Yet, in spite of such inconsistencies, Morris succeeded in what he had set out to achieve. He made young painters and architects in all countries turn to craft or design; that is, he directed them towards helping people in their everyday lives.

Why he succeeded, where Henry Cole and his friends had not, is easily seen. For one thing he practised (up to a point) what he preached. He was a fanatical craftsman himself, trying his hand at wood-carving and illumination as early as 1856, and furnishing his first rooms in London with Morris-designed and carpenter-made 'intensely medieval furniture ... as firm and as heavy as a rock'.[44] Two years later he got married, and a year after, in 1860, he moved into Red House, a house at Bexleyheath outside London, designed for him by his friend Philip Webb and furnished to Webb's and Morris's own designs. The house was daring in many ways, in exposing its red brick without a coat of stucco, in planning from inside out, that is, with secondary consideration of façades, and in frankly showing the construction inside.

9 Such a detail as the fireplace is of a truly revolutionary character, completely devoid of any period allusions and completely functional in displaying its brick courses horizontally

where the logs are laid and vertically where the smoke goes up. It is an exception in its own day and more prophetic of the coming twentieth century than anything in the field of domestic design in any country for thirty years to come. Most of the firm's early furniture is much more backward-looking, though to the simplicity of the cottage and never to the displays of the rich man's house. Yet even among the furniture sold by the firm, one can find occasional pieces of remarkably independent design. A chair designed by the Pre-Raphaelite painter Ford Madox Brown about 1860, for instance, though also clearly a simple cottage chair, shows originality in the slender elongation of the rails of the back.

Simplicity and directness unite this chair, Webb's fireplace, and the very fine designs in the flat of Morris and his firm, such as his famous *Daisy* wallpaper designed in 1862 and Webb's *Swan* tiles designed in the same year. It was the absence of simplicity and directness from the goods one could buy in the existing shops and stores which led to the creation of the

9 OPPOSITE Red House, Bexleyheath, Kent, which was designed by Philip Webb in 1859 for his friend William Morris, was comfortable, domestic, and very free in its handling of period precedent. In some details, like this fireplace, Webb shows an originality that looks forward to Voysey or Lutyens
10 RIGHT Under the influence of Morris's ideas furniture designers went back to the simplicity of the English cottage, and revived several traditional types from the country. This chair by Ford Madox Brown of about 1860, with its straight lines and rush seat, antedates the foundation of the Morris firm

11 LEFT The firm of Morris and Co. exerted a decisive influence on almost every aspect of design and interior decoration; it produced these tiles designed by Philip Webb in 1862, for a fireplace in Norman Shaw's Old Swan House (see ill. 18)
12 OPPOSITE William Morris, Peacock and Dragon curtain, 1878

firm. And there again Morris directed development both as a craftsman and a designer. When he decided that the firm should turn to the printing of textiles, and saw that bad dyeing was one of the chief troubles, he learned to dye for himself. And later, when the firm turned to tapestry weaving, he spent 516 hours in four months at the loom. But Morris's success was not only grounded in the example of craftsmanship he set, it was even more due to his genius as a designer. The designs of the Cole circle are dry and doctrinaire, Morris's are brimful of life. That is one memorable thing about them; the others are these. His designs are always crisp. There is no 'slobbering and messing about' in them.[45] Secondly, he succeeded better than anyone before or after him in achieving a balance between nature and style, between the flatness recommended for textiles, etc., by Pugin and the Cole circle, and the richness and abundance of flower and leaf as he had studied it so well in his childhood and youth. Moreover, his designs – in terms of design, not of imitation – possess the equivalent of the closeness and density of nature observed. Finally – and this matters most in our particular context – the designs, especially

13, 14

12, 14

13 Silk damask designed by Owen Jones, a friend of Henry Cole and supporter of the Great Exhibition: the Cole circle, even before Morris, reacted against the florid photographic naturalism of High Victorian designs, and produced flat patterns for flat surfaces

14 An example of Morris's own design – a chintz (*Tulip*, 1875) that shows the liveliness and crispness of Morris at his best

those of before 1876, are not in any way closely dependent on the past. They may be inspired to a certain extent by Elizabethan and Jacobean embroidery, but they are essentially original.

Just as Morris knew that to re-establish values in the things of one's everyday use was a matter of social conscience before it could ever become a matter of design, so he also knew – and in this he proved just as much a prophet – that the revival of sound architecture must precede the revival of sound design. 'Unless you are resolved', he said in 1880, 'to have good and rational architecture, it is … useless your thinking about art at all.'[46] 'The great architect' of his own day, he knew, lived a life carefully 'guarded from the common troubles of common men'.[47] What he was referring to here is the fact that the leading architects of the nineteenth century spent their lucrative working hours designing churches, public buildings and country houses and villas for the rich. This attitude changed only gradually, and it will be one of our tasks in this book to watch the change.

Its first stage is what became known as the English Domestic Revival, a turn of some architects of Morris's generation to the domestic field, entirely or almost entirely, and at the same time to a smaller scale and a greater delicacy of detail.

The two most important names are that of Morris's friend Philip Webb and that of Richard Norman Shaw. We have already met Webb more than once. An early work of his maturity is Joldwyns in Surrey of 1873. Its chief merits are a combination of boldness and straightforwardness, a refusal to do anything for show, and a great faith in local building materials. Webb, like Morris, was not a revolutionary. He loved old building in the country and used its methods and motifs. He was never afraid of mixing styles and he relished unexpected solecisms such as the long chimneys of Joldwyns, or the far-projecting five gables in a row at Standen, a house of 1892.

Shaw was a different character, more the artist, where Webb was the builder, more fanciful and elegant and perhaps also more sensitive. He, too, never departed far from the past, at

15 Norman Shaw's country houses may be compared with those of Philip Webb. Banstead, Surrey, of 1884, shows the same sensibly informal planning, though the angular chimney-stack and the neatly placed windows are more self-consciously urbane

16 A later house by Philip Webb: Standen near East Grinstead, Sussex, of 1892. Beginning as always from the requirement of comfort and convenience, Webb achieves a design combining sincerity and elegance

A Style for the Age

31

17 LEFT Shaw was an almost exact contemporary of Morris and Webb. What distinguishes him is his sophisticated wit and his willingness to play with historical styles for amusing effect. His New Zealand Chambers, in the City of London, 1872, uses motifs from the seventeenth and eighteenth century to create an efficient, well-lit office block
18 OPPOSITE Old Swan House, Chelsea, by Shaw (1876). Each of its elements can be traced to a historical source, but their combination has an elegance that is unmistakably Shaw's

18   least in his individual motifs, and he too mixed them with delight. The oversailing upper floors of Swan House, Chelsea, of 1876, are in the tradition of timber-framed building. The oriel windows on the first floor are a favourite English motif of about 1675, the excessively slender windows above are Queen Anne – but the delicate, even *piquant* ensemble is Shaw and no one else and had a great deal of influence in England and America. Shaw even introduced this novel idiom into the City of London.

17   New Zealand Chambers of 1872, unfortunately destroyed in the
      Second World War, is just as dainty and domestic. The oriel
      windows on the ground floor are specially remarkable. There
      is no period motif here; they are simply introduced to allow
      a maximum of daylight to enter the offices. Shaw's country
15   houses are nearer Webb's, although they also can perhaps be
      called more lighthearted.

19 Bedford Park, near London – the first garden suburb. The earliest houses of about 1875 were designed in a modest style that has influenced domestic architecture ever since. Gardens were large and informal; old trees were kept to give a pleasant rural feeling

There is one more respect in which Shaw's work concerns us here. At Bedford Park, not far from London, though at the time still not engulfed in the town, he built from 1875 the first garden suburb ever. The idea was not his, but Jonathan Carr's who had acquired the site. However, Shaw made it come to life, in terms of streets of modest houses and of old trees preserved in the gardens and new trees planted in the streets.

Again the design of the houses is not specially original. Their source is Tudor England and Stuart England, though again not the England of the 'prodigy houses' but of the manor house of the size of William Morris's own at Kelmscott in Oxfordshire.

Webb and Shaw had established the middle-class house as the progressive architect's chief preserve. Morris had re-established the aesthetic importance of our closest everyday surroundings. But neither he nor Webb nor Shaw had felt as strongly about the necessity of an original style of the nineteenth century, that is, about forms not taken over from the past, as Viollet-le-Duc, had done. It made little difference; for Viollet-le-Duc, when it came to designing, was if anything more period-bound than Webb and Shaw. No one in Europe could get away entirely from historicism before the 1880s.

And Europe does in fact not cover the world situation any longer at this juncture. The defeat of historicism was the work

20 Kelmscott Manor, William Morris's beloved house: the picturesque and plain outline of such old houses, with wings added gradually through the centuries, inspired English architects from Webb and Shaw onwards

21 RIGHT W. G. Low House, Bristol, Rhode Island, by Stanford White (1887, demolished). In America architects such as White and Richardson were able to break with historical precedent even more radically than Webb and Shaw
22 BELOW The F. L. Ames Memorial Gate Lodge at North Easton, Mass., by H. H. Richardson (1880–1), in his favourite massive stonework

of Americans as much as Europeans, though their front of attack was significantly broader than that of the English. In the field of the private house, H. H. Richardson and Stanford White of McKim, Mead and White showed as much fresh enterprise as Shaw, though admittedly not without knowing of his earlier houses. Occasionally, as in the house for W. G. Low at Bristol, Rhode Island, of 1887, which has been foolishly allowed to disappear, White displayed a radicalism beyond Shaw's and explicable no doubt by his pioneer background of building in a young nation. The same radicalism was applied with even greater independence in commercial architecture. It is here that America about 1890 established international leadership.

The fact that America now reached this crucial moment is one of the most memorable facts of the century. The United

22

21

States had been colonial in their reaction to European styles. They had become provincial, that is, part of a common front of progress, but an outlying part. Now all at once they left everyone else behind. They did this in first developing the skyscraper and then in finding a new style for it. In 1875 in New York the Tribune Building by Hunt rose to 79 metres (260 ft), in 1890 the Pulitzer (World) Building by Post to 114 metres (375 ft).

These early skyscrapers are simply high houses, not even especially characterized as office buildings. It would have been possible to characterize them so; for English office buildings had evolved a style as early as the 1840s in which the façade was reduced to a grid of stone piers and large windows. Chicago, a newer city than New York, and one in which traditions could not possibly matter, took up this novel and logical treatment

23

23 LEFT As early as the mid-nineteenth century English office buildings had evolved a functional style in which the wall was reduced to a grid of verticals and horizontals. This example at Nos. 5–7 Aldermanbury, London, by an unknown architect, dated from about 1840
24 OPPOSITE The Guaranty Building, Buffalo (1895) – the masterpiece of Louis Sullivan. In technique and in its strong vertical emphasis it points forward to the twentieth century, but its elaborate and complex ornament places it still in the age of Art Nouveau (see ill. 27)

and made it the standard of its skyscrapers. Moreover, Chicago added of its own the equally logical and most far-reaching innovation of applying the system of the iron frame, originally a system used for factories, to the high office building. This was first done by William Le Baron Jenney in the Home Insurance Building in 1883–5. It was an untidy and fussy building, but the tidying up was done only five or six years later by a few more talented architects: Burnham & Root, Holabird & Roche and

24

Louis Sullivan. Holabird & Roche's Tacoma Building dates from 1887–9, Burnham & Root's Monadnock Building (not a frame structure) from 1889–91, Sullivan's Wainwright Building at St Louis from 1891. In the following years appearances were rapidly even further purified. Holabird & Roche's classic

25
24

moment is the Marquette Building of 1894, Sullivan's the Guaranty Building of 1895 at Buffalo.

The importance of the School of Chicago is threefold. The job of the office building was here approached with a perfectly open mind and the functionally best solution found. An untraditional building technique offered itself to fulfil the needs of the job and was at once accepted. And it was now at last architects who took the necessary action, and no longer engineers or other outsiders. Sullivan in particular knew clearly what he was doing. In his *Ornament in Architecture*, an article of 1892, he had written: 'It would be greatly for our aesthetic good, if we should refrain entirely from the use of ornament for a period of years, in order that our thought might concentrate … upon the production of buildings … comely in the nude.'[48] Yet Sullivan himself loved ornament, though he used it externally only in a few judiciously chosen places. It is a very personal feathery foliage ornament, inspired partly by the Morris

26, 27

Movement, but much freer, wilder and more entangled. It has been called Art Nouveau or Proto-Art Nouveau, and whether such a term is justifiable cannot be decided until Art Nouveau has been closely examined.

This is in fact our task now; for Art Nouveau was the other campaign to drive out historicism. This is its primary

25 OPPOSITE The Marquette Building, Chicago, by Holabird & Roche. Here in 1894 the steel frame is completely expressed around large, broad windows (those at the bottom are already the 'Chicago type', see ill. 179), the detailing is plain, and the whole is so well planned it is still highly efficient today

26, 27 Cast-iron ornament by Louis Sullivan (opposite) on the Guaranty Building (1895, see ill. 24) and (above) on the Carson Pirie Scott store (begun 1899, ill. 179). Ornament in architecture had a special importance for Sullivan, and his own, with its tensions and exuberant curls, is strikingly original

significance in European design and architecture, whatever other delights and aberrations it may harbour. Among the sources of modern architecture and design it is still the most controversial. Today's architecture and design having taken a turn away from rationalism and towards fancy, Art Nouveau has suddenly become topical, and the very qualities of it which in this narrative will appear historically most dubious are hailed. Books and exhibitions have vied with each other to present its fascination. All the more important must it be to attempt an analysis – aesthetic as well as historical.

28 Mackmurdo's title-page for his book of 1883 defending Wren's City Churches introduced motifs which became popular throughout Europe

Chapter 2
Art Nouveau

The term Art Nouveau comes from S. Bing's shop in Paris opened late in 1895, the corresponding German term *Jugendstil* from a journal which began to appear in 1896. But the style is older. Traditionally it is supposed to have started fully mature in Victor Horta's house, no. 6 rue Paul-Emile Janson in Brussels, and that house was designed in 1892 and built in 1893. But it marks no more than the transfer of the style from the small to a larger scale and from design to architecture.

The *incunabula* of Art Nouveau belong to the years 1883–8. They are the following. Arthur H. Mackmurdo, wealthy young architect and designer, in 1883 wrote a book on Sir Christopher Wren's churches in the City of London – not a subject that seems to call for Art Nouveau – and gave it a title-page fully Art Nouveau. What justifies this statement? The area inside the frame is filled by a non-repeating, asymmetrical pattern of tulips, stylized vigorously into flaming shapes. To the left and right sharply cut short by the frame are two cockerels, pulled out to an excessive thinness and length. The characteristics which we shall see recur whenever we speak of Art Nouveau are the asymmetrical flaming shape derived from nature, and handled with a certain wilfulness or bravado, and the refusal to accept any ties with the past. Of course Mackmurdo's design is not without ancestors, but they are not to be found among the hallowed period styles.

He must have looked at Morris and, like Morris, at the Pre-Raphaelites. He must have known William Blake, as the Pre-Raphaelites did, but he was also familiar – socially too – with Whistler, and although Whistler was an Impressionist in his formative years, he soon found an aim of his own, the aim to blend the light, soft, hazy tones of Impressionism with the creation of *piquant* decorative patterns, sometimes

29 ABOVE AND RIGHT Three trends after 1860: (top right) seeming naturalism pleasantly formalized in the signet of Morris and Co. (c. 1861); (bottom right) sinuous elegance in Mackmurdo's signet for the Century Guild, incorporating its initials CG (1884); (above) Japanese stylization in Whistler's calligraphic Butterfly signature

30 OPPOSITE The Peacock Room, 1876–7: lavish decoration by Whistler in blue and gold 'Japonaiserie' of a room designed by Thomas Jeckyll for the shipping magnate F. R. Leyland's collection of porcelain

30
29
almost abstract, sometimes linear as in the celebrated Peacock Room of 1876–7. His equally celebrated signet, the butterfly, is an example of his genius for witty stylization. Companions are Morris's early signet of his firm and Mackmurdo's of the Century Guild which he started in 1882. The three signets sum up a story of nature and abstraction in which Morris, Whistler and Mackmurdo are of equal importance. It need hardly be added that the idea of calling a firm a guild was a bow to the Ruskin and Morris circle. It was to convey connotations of the Middle Ages and of cooperation instead of exploitation or competition. Mackmurdo's guild brought out a journal

31
the *Hobby Horse*, and the title-page and typography of this also are worth remembering. It preceded by six years Morris's more famous venture into typography and book-making, the Kelmscott Press. Mackmurdo designed textiles for his guild

31 Title page of the *Hobby Horse*, designed by Selwyn Image in 1884. Printed on hand-made paper in a carefully chosen traditional typeface, it heralded a style of book-design lasting well into this century. 'Never before', said *The Studio*, 'had modern printing been treated as a serious art.'

in 1884 too, and they possess much of the originality and the swagger of the Wren title. It is difficult to assess the effects of the Century Guild. The eighties were the years of Morris's wide success as a designer. His by then much more staid, symmetrical, as it were, classic designs for textiles were the principal influence in England. But Mackmurdo's daring also found an echo here and there. Heywood Sumner, who was indeed for a while associated with the Guild, worked in its style. The cover of the translation of Fouqué's *Undine* (1888) is a masterpiece in its own right. The world of sprites or fairies of the water was bound to appeal to Art Nouveau sensibility. Hair and waves and sea-weeds were as alluring as such elemental creatures themselves, not guided by reason but by instinct. For order enforced by intellect is one of the things against which Art Nouveau was in opposition, and the conscious selection of styles of the past to be imitated represented that principle of enforced order.

32 Cover of Fouqué's *Undine* by Heywood Sumner, 1888

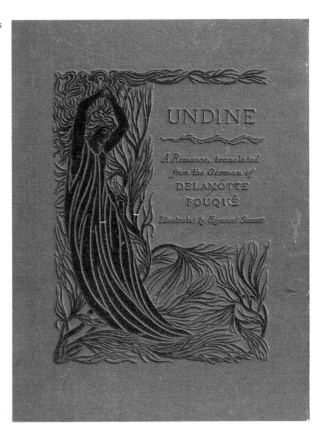

33, 34 ABOVE AND OPPOSITE The beginnings of Art Nouveau: printed cotton fabrics (c. 1882), above, Textile length, right, *Peacock*, by Arthur Heygate Mackmurdo, partly derived from Morris but containing all the elements of the later style. They were printed by Simpson and Godlee of Manchester for the Century Guild

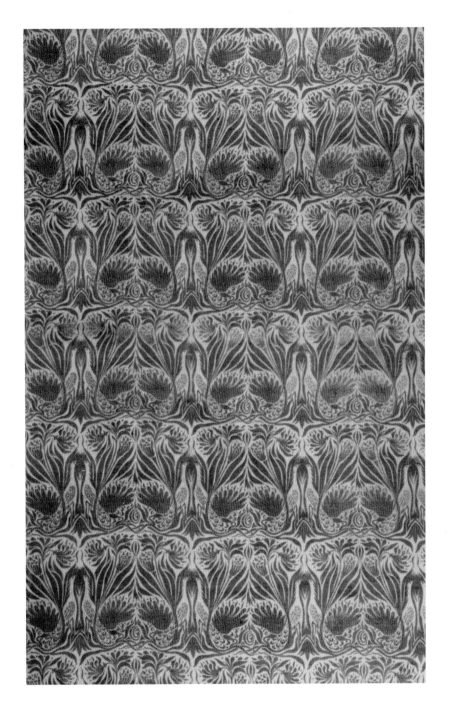

35, 36 In glass the
Art Nouveau created
novel shapes as well as
novel decoration. Among
its pioneers was Eugène
Rousseau, with such pieces
as a vase with Klee-like
scratched decoration, 1884
(right) and a carp vase,
1878–84 (above)

37 A vase of shaded coloured glass by Emile Gallé, of about 1896. Gallé, like Obrist (ill. 55) had studied botany

Mackmurdo's exploration was one in two dimensions, as indeed Morris's had been. But efforts at breaking the shackles of historicism in the crafts, expressing themselves in the shaping not the decorating of objects, were not entirely lacking either. Pride of place here goes to France. Emile Gallé of Nancy was five years older than Mackmurdo. His glass vessels of 1884 and after are as alien to nineteenth-century conventions as Mackmurdo's book and textile designs, with their soft, subtle colours and the mystery of their naturalistically-represented

37   flowers emerging out of cloudy grounds. Nor was Gallé alone, even in these earliest years. Eugène Rousseau, for instance, a much older craftsman in Paris of whom too little is known, turned to a new style at the same time. The Musée des Arts Décoratifs bought certain pieces from him in 1885, and among

35, 36   them is a *jardinière* in imitation of jade and a tall vase of clear glass, both strikingly independent and courageous. The scratched-in pattern of the tall vase is particularly bold – Klee rather than Morris. E. B. Leveillé, a pupil of Rousseau, showed glass at the Paris Exhibition of 1889, wholly in the same spirit,

38   for instance a vase of *craquelé* glass marbled in green and red. In ceramics there is only one parallel to Rousseau, and that takes us to the most influential of all outsiders, to Gauguin.

38 ABOVE Crackleware goblet by Ernest Baptiste Leveillé (c. 1889); marbled with colour both inside and out, and only about 15 cm (6 inches) high
39 OPPOSITE Crystal vase decorated with translucent enamel, about 20 cm (9 inches) high, by Emile Gallé (1887)

40 The only leading painter to experiment with crafts at this time was Gauguin: he carved and painted this cabinet with panels in 1881 for his own dining-room

41 Gauguin also designed a ceramic centrepiece for a table, in the form of a girl bathing in a pool 1888

42 A pitcher by Gauguin, baked and enamelled in 1886 by Chaplet

Gauguin is the only one of the leading painters who not only influenced design by his forms but experimented with crafts himself. In 1881, before he had given up his job at the bank to devote himself to art, he decorated a cupboard in his dining-room with carved wooden panels in decidedly exotic shapes and painted red, green, yellow and brown. Primitivism starts from here, and a primitivism very different from Philip Webb's. Webb went back to the English countryside, Gauguin already here to barbarity. Then, in 1886 he turned to pottery. The jug here illustrated is as original and as ruthlessly crude. The épergne with the bathing girl of 1888 is a little less uncompromising. In fact, the introduction of the female

40

42
41

figure into objects for use was both in the nineteenth-century tradition and to the liking of Art Nouveau.

Where Gauguin comes closest to the Mackmurdo-Sumner endeavours is in his work in two dimensions, that is, as a painter and a graphic artist. The catalogue title-page for the Café Volpini exhibition of 1889 is violently primitive again, a painting such as the *Man with the Axe* has the vermiculating lines which became a hall-mark of Art Nouveau. Their influence was brief but wide, and not only on painters such as Munch. Gauguin conveyed his concern with craft as well as his style to his friends of Pont-Aven, and so we find Emile Bernard in 1888 doing wood-carving as well as an appliqué wall-hanging, and

43

45

46

43 ABOVE Gauguin's *Aux Roches Noires* of 1889, from the catalogue of an exhibition of impressionist and synthetic painting at the Café Volpini in Paris
44 LEFT The serpentine line of the water ripples in Gauguin's *Man with the Axe*, painted in Tahiti in 1891, reappear in Henry van de Velde's title-page design for *Dominical*, of 1892
45 OPPOSITE *Man with the Axe* by Paul Gauguin, 1891

46 OPPOSITE Emile Bernard, also one of the Pont-Aven circle, made this wall-hanging of Breton women picking pears in c. 1890
47 ABOVE Among Gauguin's friends at Pont-Aven many were roused by his example to take up crafts. The Danish painter Jens Ferdinand Willumsen produced this vase in the form of a mother, father and baby (1891)

47   J. F. Willumsen in 1890 turning to ceramics very much of the Gauguin kind. Willumsen stayed in France and then returned to Denmark. There, however, while he had been away, a parallel development had begun in ceramics, independent, it seems of Pont-Aven. Thorvald Bindesbøll, two years older than Gauguin, and an architect by training, the son in fact of the most original Danish architect of the neo-Greek movement, had in the 1880s begun to work in ceramics. The plate of 1891 with its crudely

drawn tulips asymmetrically and indeed casually arranged still links up with Gauguin and Art Nouveau; his later plates stand entirely on their own in the whole of Europe. One is tempted to see in them a parallel to the Kandinsky moment in art; but they antedate it by nearly twenty years. One might also – and more justly – look in the direction of Gaudi, but even then Bindesbøll seems to retain priority. Bindesbøll's impact remains, and what ties him into our particular context here, is the attitude of the architect turning potter and indeed craftsman in general.

48
49

48 BELOW The Dane Thorvald Bindesbøll became the most original ceramic artist of his generation. The dish, of 1891, is still Art Nouveau in its twisting lines, naturalistic tulips and asymmetry, though there are influences from the East
49 OPPOSITE A later dish by Bindesbøll of 1899, with its bold abstract decoration, places him in a class apart from every other artist in Europe at the time. Both the dishes shown here are glazed ceramic with *sgraffito* decoration and both are large – about 45 cm (18 inches) in diameter

62   Chapter 2

50 LEFT The greatest English master of Art Nouveau sculpture was Alfred Gilbert; on the base of the 'Eros' fountain in Piccadilly Circus (1892) he freely indulged his taste for writhing, marine, slightly sinister forms

51 OPPOSITE Silver table-centre with inlays of mother-of-pearl, designed by Gilbert for Queen Victoria's Golden Jubilee in 1887 and presented to her by her officers. It stands over 1 metre (3 feet) high

No radicalism of Bindesbøll's force can be found anywhere else. The nearest to it in England is certain half-concealed elements in the highly successful monuments of Alfred Gilbert. Gilbert was a sculptor in metals, precious metals on a small scale, bronze in his large works, monuments as a rule. Their figures are embedded in a gristly, crustaceous substance, some of it seemingly in a heavy flow like lava, some arrested in grotesque shapes. There was only one man in another country as ready and perhaps readier to force metal into such violent expression: Antoni Gaudí, whom we shall meet more prominently soon. The material of his first challenges was iron. His father was a coppersmith; and he grew up day in day out seeing metal molten and shaped. Inspiration to experiment with iron for decorative purposes will also have

50, 51

52 Wrought-iron grille of Gaudí's early Casa Vicens, c. 1880, based on palm
fronds; the son of a coppersmith, Gaudí used metalwork lavishly

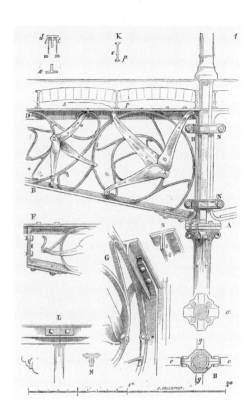

53 Detail from Viollet-le-Duc's *Entretiens* (1872), demonstrating cast-iron construction and the use of iron foliage in a spandrel

come from Viollet-le-Duc's *Entretiens*, which show in the details of spandrels between iron arches how medievalizing foliage trails can be made of iron. Gaudí's first house, the Casa Vicens at Barcelona, of 1878–80, is medievalizing too, though in a fantastical semi-Moorish way, and fantastical also are the spiky palm-fronds or stars of the iron fence. In the Palau Güell of 1885–9, his first major job, the forms are less aggressive and more ingratiating, and the parabolic shape of the portal is as unexpected and free from references to the past as are the undulations of the iron. The ease of bending wrought iron and its ductility, which allow for the most delicate stalk-like filaments, made iron a favourite material of Art Nouveau.

It came into its own at once with Horta's house of 1892–3 already referred to (p. 43). The famous staircase of no. 6 rue Paul-Emile Janson has a slender iron column left exposed, an iron handrail of thin tendril-like curves, and in addition, not of iron, applied wall, floor and ceiling decoration of the same curves. One can hardly believe that this could have been designed without influence from the England of Mackmurdo.

53
52
108

88

Indirect influence from Pont-Aven is more easily proved, as we shall see presently. Although we are dealing with architecture here, the job on the staircase was essentially one of decorating, like Gaudí's at the entrance to the Palau Güell. We are not sufficiently prepared yet for the architecture proper of both buildings and their designers.

Art Nouveau is indeed very largely a matter of decoration – so much so that some have denied its validity as an architectural style – and it is furthermore largely a matter of surface decoration. We must now follow it through the years of its conquest and international success – a short-lived success; for it began about 1893, and it was faced with a formidable opposition from about 1900 onwards. After 1905 it held out only in a few countries, and mostly in commercial work in which no creative impetus was left, if there ever had been any.

As textiles and the art of the book initiated the movement, they may be considered first. Henry van de Velde, Belgian painter, influenced by the *pointillistes* and by Gauguin, turned to design about 1890, the first such case of conversion by Morris that we can watch closely. The tapestry, or rather *appliqué* wall hanging, called *Angels' Watch*, of 1891, can only be understood as an echo of the work of Bernard. It interests us because the disposition of the forms and the all-pervading undulations make it so thoroughly Art Nouveau. The trees are stylized more rigorously than the figures. A year or two later Hermann Obrist did that curious piece of embroidery which is inspired by flowers with their root. It is a *tour de force*, and if one compares it with the best work in the field of textiles in England during the same years, the work of Charles F. Annesley Voysey, a first impression is obtained of the restraint and the sanity of England during those years. Excesses of Art Nouveau are all but absent. One exception to this rule has already been named: Alfred Gilbert; the other – Scottish and not English – will be commented on later. Voysey's textiles of about 1890 are clearly influenced by Mackmurdo's, but they are milder in their rhythms and a little more accommodating. Less than ten years later Voysey was to abandon this style altogether and turn to another, more original, but less Art Nouveau.

54 OPPOSITE ABOVE *The Angels' Watch* by the Belgian designer Henry van de Velde (1892–93), no doubt inspired by the Pont-Aven group. This is the essence of Art Nouveau – a recognizable subject, but every outline reduced to undulation
55 OPPOSITE BELOW Obrist's embroidery *Whiplash* (1895), like an exotic botanical plate, shows one plant's leaves, bud, flower and root. Obrist had studied botany, and looked to art to 'glorify nature never seen till now, its powerful life and gigantic divine forces'

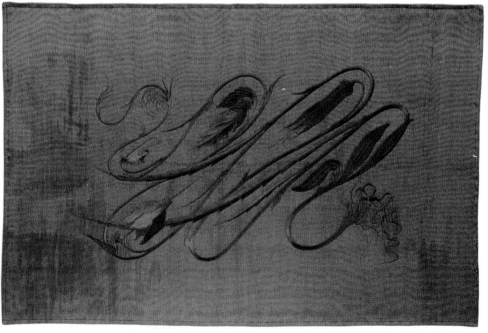

56 ABOVE 'It was as if spring had come all of a sudden,' said Van de Velde when he first saw designs by Voysey. This design for a wallpaper showing dragons and flames is an exuberant design of 1882. Voysey is in the line of Morris and Mackmurdo, but Art Nouveau transforms his early designs into something quite distinct
57 OPPOSITE Voysey's *Tulip*, a print of 1893–95

58 Georges Lemmen's catalogue for an exhibition of *Les Vingt* (1891) is closer to the boldness and vigour of Gauguin than to the sophistication of his fellow-Belgian Horta

In typography Belgium again held a key position. *Les Vingt*, that adventurous club of artists whose exhibitions were perhaps the most courageous in Europe – they had shown Gauguin in 1889, Van Gogh in 1890, books and works of English artist-craftsmen in 1892 – had as the title-page of its catalogue in 1891 a design by Georges Lemmen reflecting Gauguin at his most Art Nouveau. The year after, Van de Velde went into book decoration. His title-page to Max Elskamp's *Dominical* is uncannily close to the Gauguin of the *Man with the Axe*, painted in Tahiti the year before. Of 1896 are the initials made for *Van Nu en Straks*, delightful play with the typical swelling and tapering curves of Gauguin as well as the English book artists in the Mackmurdo succession. Here again the contrast to the staid splendour of the Kelmscott Press is great and can serve as a reminder of how differently things were to go in England. Germany joined in the new Belgian style after a few years' hesitation. Otto Eckmann who died young in 1902 and Peter Behrens who soon repented these wild oats were the leading designers. Eckmann left painting for design in 1894, Behrens in 1895. Both designed type-faces of Art Nouveau character about 1900 and also book decoration, printed matter for business firms, book jackets, bindings and so on.

58

44

45

59

60, 61

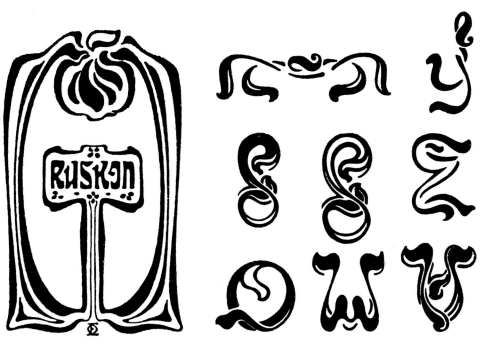

59-61 The typographic revival begun by Mackmurdo (ill. 28) and Morris was carried on in Belgium by Van de Velde with these free, scrolly initials for his magazine *Van Nu en Straks*, of 1896 (above right; see also ill. 44). In Germany Otto Eckmann designed this alphabet and cover for Ruskin's *Seven Lamps of Architecture* (above), both about 1900

ABCDEFGHIJK
LMNOPQRSTU
VWXYZ
abcdefghijklmn
opqrsítuvwxyz
chck 1234567890

A remark on book-binding itself must be appended to these remarks on the art of the book. The reason for picking out, as one of the examples to be illustrated, a binding by the Nancy craftsman René Wiener is that it introduces us to a different aspect of Art Nouveau. The asymmetric and the curving, curly shapes which were *de rigueur* could be obtained abstractly or naturalistically. Van de Velde believed as fervently in the one, as the artists of Nancy believed in the other. Neither was wholly original. Henry Cole and his friends had preached the necessity of ornament being 'rather abstractive than … imitative',[49] the Victorian decorators themselves in all countries had wallowed in accurately portrayed roses, cabbage leaves and all the rest. Now Gallé had an inscription above the door to his studio which read: 'Our roots are in the depths of the woods, beside the springs, upon the mosses', and wrote in an article:

62 Bookbinding too was affected by the new ideas: one of its masters was René Wiener of Nancy, who produced this portfolio for engravings – decorated with vines and a press – designed and made by Camille Martin in 1893

63 Binding by Wiener for Flaubert's *Salammbô* (1893), with enamelled corners by Camille Martin. Victor Prouvé, who did the leather-work, designed it to suggest the contents of Flaubert's novel, which he had long admired: it shows Moloch, the moon-goddess Tanit, and Salammbô writhing in the python's embrace

'The forms furnished by plants adapt themselves quite naturally to line-work.'[50] Line is the operative word. In the mid-nineteenth century, naturalism reigned in all fields; the natural sciences were worshipped. Even in a church, otherwise imitated accurately from the style of say the thirteenth century, the foliage of the capitals was made yet more real than it had been at any moment in the Middle Ages, and the leaves of native trees and hedgerows were displayed proudly. Art Nouveau designers went to nature because they were in need of forms to express growth, not of human making, organic not crystalline forms, sensuous not intellectual forms.

So much for Nancy – and of course others in other countries. Van de Velde on the other hand insisted on the intellectual process of converting nature to make it ornament. Ornament, he said, must be 'structural and dynamographic'. 'The least naturalistic association' would menace the eternal values of ornament.[51] Few were as radical as Van de Velde, but as a matter of principle, Voysey, for instance, agreed: 'To go to nature is

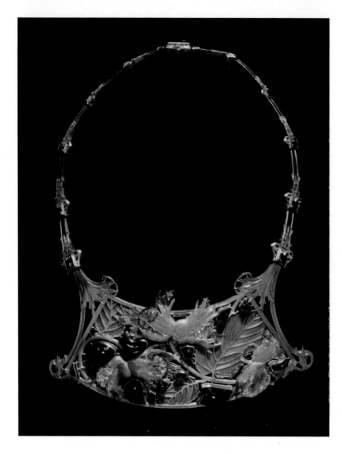

64 LEFT A necklace (1900), also by Lalique, is a filigree design of hazel-nuts and foliage in low relief, with translucent enamels and diamonds

65 OPPOSITE Art Nouveau jewelry offered the greatest opportunity for fantasy. In René Lalique's pendant of 1901 naturalistic and stylized shapes are inextricably combined. The flowing lines are at once the stems of flowers and a woman's hair; at the bottom, like some exotic fruit, hangs a pearl

of course to go to the fountain head, but ... before a living plant a man must go through an elaborate process of selection and analysis. The natural forms have to be reduced to mere symbols.'[52] The future was with the abstractionists not the naturalists, even if not the immediate future. For as soon as Art Nouveau spread and became commercially exploitable, its Van de Velde version was too exacting, and the less pure mixtures of curvaceous ornament with the curvaceous forms of plants or indeed the female body, were certain of a greater success.

The years of universal success, at least on the continent of Europe, were the ending years of the nineteenth and the very first years of the twentieth century. The catalogue of the Paris Exhibition of 1900 is a mine of Art Nouveau. The necklace with pendant by René Lalique was shown, and it illustrates, as do Lalique's pendant and brooch, the part played by nature and the part by stylization in Art Nouveau. From Germany came the

64
65

66 LEFT A brooch by Wilhelm Lucas von Cranach combines many favourite Art Nouveau motifs – insects, sea-creatures, intertwining lines and an atmosphere of corruption and menace – to show a butterfly strangled by an octopus
67 ABOVE A brooch by Lalique (c. 1898–99) in the form of a peacock, its enamelled gold tail set with moonstones

66 brooch by Wilhelm Lucas von Cranach. It represents an octopus strangling a butterfly, though it can just as well be seen abstractly and is perhaps seen in that way to greater advantage. It is an exquisite display of red, green and blue enamel with baroque pearls and small precious and semi-precious stones. In Lalique's brooch the enamelled peacock's neck rises out of feathers of gold
67 and moonstone. With jewelry we have moved from Art Nouveau in two dimensions to Art Nouveau in the round. There was no reason why the principle of eternal undulations should not be applied to three dimensions. All materials were indeed affected.
70 In Victor Prouvé's bronze bowl *Night* of 1894 flowing hair takes the place of Mackmurdo's or Obrist's stalks and leaves, Lalique's feathers and Cranach's tentacles. Every time what tempted the craftsman were natural elements lending themselves to Art Nouveau sinuosity.

Ceramics and especially glass were ideal media for Art
68 Nouveau. Georges Hoentschel's dark brown earthenware vase of *c.* 1901 with the off-whites of its daringly accidental running-down glaze is an example of the former; the brothers Daum's bottle-shaped vase of 1893 with crocuses at the bottom and the glaze running down the high neck, and of course the famous Favrile
71 glass of Louis C. Tiffany are examples of the latter. Tiffany also began as a painter. He turned to decorative and stained glass, and in 1893 started a glass blowing department. The swaying, exceedingly attenuated forms of his vases and their subtle, never wholly calculated, shot colours made them a pattern for Europe
72 as well, and Karl Koepping's glass – Koepping again was a painter at first – is clearly in the first place inspired by Tiffany's.

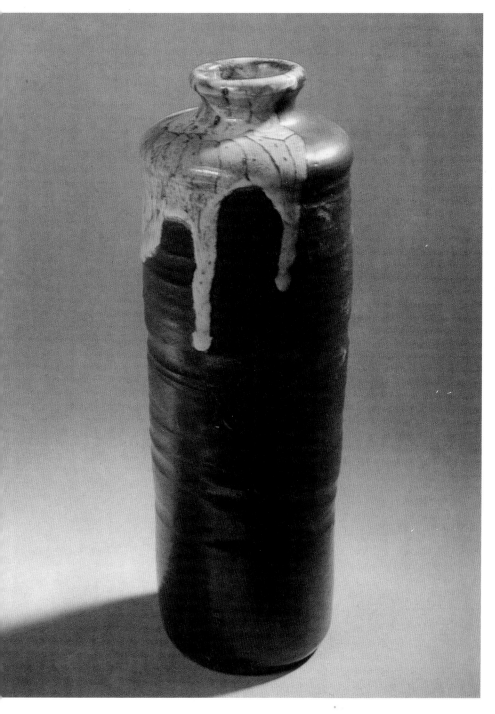

68 Brown-glazed earthenware vase by Georges Hoentschel of about 1901:
the creamy overglaze is allowed to drip down at random

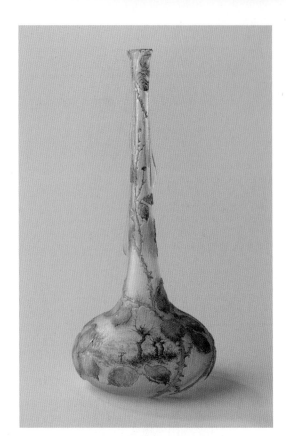

69 RIGHT A vase of c. 1895
with a winter landscape by the
brothers Daum
70 BELOW Bronze bowl by
Victor Prouvé (see ill. 74):
Night, 1894. In the flowing hair
tiny figures are tossed as if on
waves of the sea

71, 72 Glass was drawn into the shapes
of Art Nouveau. Tiffany (below, a
vase of 1897–98) made it iridescent;
Koepping's wine-glasses are flowers
(right), their bowls held between leaves
on frail stems

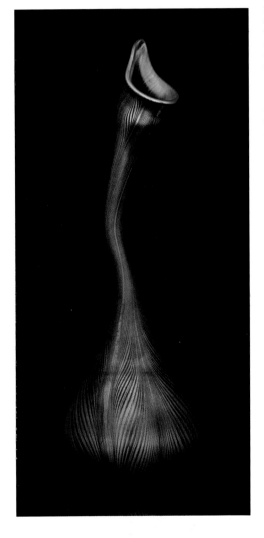

Art Nouveau

Wood is a less tractable material, and much Art Nouveau furniture suffers from the conflict between its nature and the expressive desire of Art Nouveau. One way to avoid the conflict was to confine the decoration to curves on flat surfaces. But as a rule, and most dedicatedly in France, the material was forced to obey the style. France, in fact, is the country which in the end carried on longest in Art Nouveau. There were two centres: Paris, of course, and Nancy. That a provincial capital should vie with the national capital was an improbable thing to happen in so metropolitan a civilization as that of the rising twentieth century. However, the case is matched by that of Glasgow. Nancy is the town of Gallé and of a group of other craftsmen-manufacturers all at first affected by Gallé's faith in nature as the source of ornament. Louis Majorelle's is the most familiar name after Gallé's. It is characteristic of the efforts needed to make Art Nouveau furniture that he used to model his pieces in clay before they were made of timber.

75, 77

73 BELOW Simplicity and solidity: William Morris's ideals, represented by his own patterns and Philip Webb's oak furniture (after 1858). The rushseated chairs (see also ill. 10) were especially popular in the 1870s and after
74 OPPOSITE Excess and artifice: dining-room of cedar by Eugène Vallin for a client at Nancy (1903–6). The leather panels, ceiling and sideboard carvings are by Prouvé, the glass by Daum, and the copper chandelier by Vallin himself

Art Nouveau like the Baroque made claims to the
Gesamtkunstwerk. Only rarely can one do justice to an
individual piece without knowing of its intended context.
That alone debarred it or should have debarred it from
quantity production. With the vandalism typical of sons
against the generation of their fathers, most of the Art Nouveau
ensembles have been destroyed. It is lucky that the Musée
de l'Ecole de Nancy could reassemble, even if not without
alteration and reductions, a complete dining-room by Eugène
Vallin. This was begun only in 1903, at a moment when the
other leading countries were already moving away from Art
Nouveau. In looking at this room and trying it out as a place to
live in, one can understand why. Such violent expression tires
one soon. Furniture ought to be a background. Here we feel
intruders. Also there is the constant clash between function
and form – table legs awkwardly lumpy at the foot, doors and
shelf recess of bosomy shape. And finally, one may well worry
about wood made to perform ceramic or metallic curves.

74

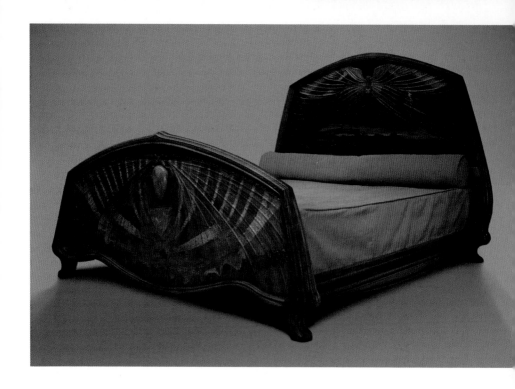

One of the most daring cases is the music room by Alexandre
Charpentier, a sculptor before he became a decorator. The
76   music-stand illustrated is a pure example of the three-dimensional
Art Nouveau curve, spatially ingenious and functionally dubious.
Charpentier belonged to the Parisian group *Les Cinq*, soon (by
the accession of Plumet) to become *Les Six*. They formed one
centre of the crafts revival in Paris, the other was Bing's shop
L'Art Nouveau, a more international centre of course. Among
the designers specially connected with Bing, Eugène Gaillard in
78   his later work showed one French way out of the impasse of Art
Nouveau. He said already in 1906 that furniture should express its
function, that it should be in harmony with the material and that
curves should be used decoratively only. His furniture is indeed
a return to the principles and forms of the most refined French
eighteenth-century furniture, even if he never stooped to imitation.

After these French pieces Van de Velde's great desk of 1896 is
79   impressive in its radicalism and its tautness. There is neither
the elephantine massiveness of Vallin's dining room nor
Gaillard's half-concealed sympathy with the classic past. Van
de Velde impressed Germany much when he first showed in
1897. Indeed Germany started a little later than Belgium and

75 OPPOSITE Emile Gallé's great Butterfly Bed of 1904, which again shows the fashion for insects, was his last work. He watched its completion from an invalid chair and died in the same year
76 RIGHT Alexandre Charpentier went further still in this swirling music-stand of hornbeam, part of an ensemble of 1901. Both designs would be more suitable for metal or plastic

77 LEFT Louis Majorelle modelled his furniture in clay, and the freedom thus obtained is evident in his table (1902) of mahogany, tamarind and gilded bronze

78 ABOVE The more chaste furniture of Eugène Gaillard, such as this pearwood canapé, paraphrases classic French furniture in Art Nouveau language
79 OPPOSITE ABOVE A desk by Henry van de Velde, 1898–99 – clean and functional in its general effect in spite of the opulent Art Nouveau curves
80, 81 OPPOSITE BELOW Armchairs by Otto Eckmann (1900, left) and Richard Riemerschmid (1903, right)

France, but for a short time men of strong personality joined Art Nouveau and produced outstanding work. Otto Eckmann, better known as a typographer and decorator of books,

80   designed furniture for the Grand Duke of Hessen about 1898, surprisingly structural, considering his free use of natural forms in the books he decorated. The solution of the seeming contradiction must be Van de Velde. Richard Riemerschmid's

81   chairs are more English in their inspiration, and he was indeed among those who, when he turned away from Art Nouveau, did so for social as well as aesthetic reasons. The greatest ornamental originality in Germany was August Endell's, as we shall see in another context later. What is known of his

82, 83, 84 LEFT AND OPPOSITE Furniture
with a genuine sculptural quality
– restrained in Endell's armchair
of 1899 (left), completely free in
Gaudí's chairs for the Casa Calvet
of 1896–1904 (opposite below).
Gaudí's benches for Sta Coloma de
Cervelló (opposite above; see also
ill. 104) stand like insects on their
rough iron legs

82

furniture has a curious plastic quality – plastic in the true
English sense of the word – quite different from anything so
far examined. The scrolls at the ends of the arms of the chair
illustrated are particularly convincing, both aesthetically and
functionally.

84

Only one other designer of furniture did likewise, and he
was neither German nor French nor English, nor indeed a
furniture designer. Antoni Gaudí's chairs for the Casa Calvet of
1896–1904 have the same qualities as Endell's but driven to an
extreme. They are Art Nouveau in that they shun the straight
line, shun all relation to the past and also in that they are
fanatically personal. The bone-like formation of the elements is
all Gaudí's. His most surprising furniture is that for the chapel
of the Colonia Güell at Santa Coloma de Cervelló on which he

83

worked from 1898 till 1914. Here is one of the few cases of design
trying to do what painting was doing at the same moment, that
is, scrapping all the agreed conventions of art. The brutality of

85 ABOVE Porch of the crypt of Sta Coloma de Cervelló, by Gaudí (1898–1914). The materials are rough stone, brick, cement, columnar basalt (pillar on the left), and tiles laid edge to edge in the vaults. Details were devised on the spot rather than at the drawing-board
86 OPPOSITE Gaudí covered the writhing benches that surrounded the Güell Park with brilliant chips of tile, creating a restless, playful landscape

the iron undercarriage of these benches, especially the feet, and of the seats themselves, goes indeed beyond Art Nouveau.

Gaudí's architecture poses even more urgently the problem of how far Art Nouveau as a term with an analysable, useful meaning can be stretched. That he is first and foremost Gaudí there can be no question. The ironwork of the Casa Vicens and the portal of the Palau Güell have already demonstrated that. But that his views and those of Art Nouveau coincided in many ways is patent.

52
108

However, there is a greater problem involved here. It has been denied by more than one scholar that Art Nouveau architecture exists at all. It has been argued that Art Nouveau was no more than a decorative fashion, lasting hardly more than ten years and hence not deserving the attention it has recently been given. None of these contentions can be maintained. It might be worth looking at a number of exteriors and interiors of buildings in a systematic order culminating in Gaudí. The best start is Endell's

87 In the Atelier Elvira (1896, destroyed in 1944) August Endell was obviously influenced by Horta's stair (ill. 88); the staircase seems to float up like the stem of some water-plant surrounded by tendrils, with an unexpected accent in the spiky spray of the light fixture

88 In the staircase of no. 6 rue Paul-Emile Janson (1892–3), in Brussels, Horta exploited both the strength of iron – in the supporting column – and its malleability, in the free-flowing lines of the handrail and 'capital' which are repeated in paint and mosaic

89 The façade of the Atelier Elvira, Munich, by August Endell. The large reliefs in red and turquoise stucco, window shapes and twisted glazing-bars set the flat surface in motion

Atelier Elvira in Munich, unfortunately not preserved. A flat façade is made Art Nouveau primarily, it is true, by means of a huge abstract ornament of a crustaceous kind, but surely not only by this. The asymmetrical fenestration, the tops of the windows and doorway like looped-up curtains and the glazing bars all play their part. And when you entered the house, a stair hall received you in which all the forms undulated, and not only those applied to the walls. The handrail of the staircase, the newel post and light fitting rocketing up from the post – all this is architectural, that is, three-dimensional and articulating inner space. That the famous and at the time publicized staircase in Horta's house in the rue Paul-Emile Janson was the pattern is evident, and that staircase with its slender iron pillar also is genuinely architectural. Admittedly exteriors were not often up to the novelties of the interiors – as had been the case

90 ABOVE Horta, the leading Art Nouveau architect of Belgium, built the Hôtel Solvay for a wealthy client between 1895 and 1900. The façade is a complex arrangement of flat and curved surfaces, with the ornament seeming to grow out of the material
91 OPPOSITE Inside, the stair again has Horta's brilliant ironwork (even the studs are part of the design), and stained glass in the same mood

92 ABOVE Horta's own house, in the rue Américaine, Brussels (1898–9): iron supports curl-like tendrils around the balconies, and the pillars leaf out as in his earlier stair (ill. 88)
93 OPPOSITE Auditorium of Horta's Maison du Peuple (designed in 1896 as a vast social centre): the iron framework is fully exposed, but softened by Horta's genius for curving metalwork

of the Atelier Elvira – but if one looks at the façade of Horta's
90, 92 own house of 1898–9, or the former Hôtel Solvay of 1895–1900,
one sees again the same spindliness of iron supports, the same
play of pliable iron decoration round them and the same sense
of transparency as inside.

Altogether, the role of iron in Art Nouveau is interesting
enough to deserve a paragraph. Iron is a decorative as well as
a structural material. Viollet-le-Duc had recognized that and
suggested its use in both capacities in the same buildings.
53 He was the fountain head. Then, and independent of him,
iron and later steel, externally in conjunction with glass,
became the most technically suitable material for the factory,
the warehouse and the office building. The quality which
recommended it was that it lent itself to the unmitigated
grid. This was an argument in itself not of an aesthetic
nature, though the twentieth century discovered the aesthetic
possibilities of the grid. But Art Nouveau must retain the credit
for the discovery of the aesthetic possibilities of iron and glass –
even if these qualities have nothing to do with those of the grid.
Art Nouveau adored lightness, attenuation, transparency and
of course sinuosity. Iron meant thin members and ductility;
iron and glass used externally produced the same transparency
93, 94 obtained internally by iron alone. Horta's Maison du Peuple
of 1896–9 was the Art Nouveau version of the American office
building – both dependent on iron, but in exactly opposite ways.
In America the steel controls structure and thereby appearance,

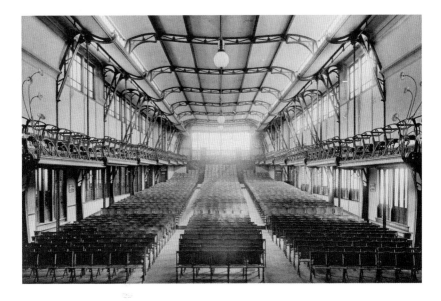

94 OPPOSITE Façade of
the Maison du Peuple in
Brussels, by Horta (1896–9,
demolished in 1965–6), with
curving walls of iron and
glass between brick panels
95 RIGHT Sehring's Tietz
Department Store in Berlin
of 1898 included vast
walls of iron-framed glass;
the masonry sections are
conventional neo-Baroque

though the façades are of stone cladding the steel; in the
Maison du Peuple the iron frame is visible, and iron provides
the music playing round the frame and embroidering on the
eternal Art Nouveau theme of the curve which also is that of the
façade as a whole. The rhythm of iron, glass, steel and brick is
restless and the building does not read as a whole. In the great
hall inside, iron is exposed everywhere, and yet the effect is not
utilitarian, largely again thanks to the use of curving members.
The most daringly glazed commercial building of those years
was Bernhard Sehring's Tietz Department Store in Berlin of
1898, which consists of three broad stone bays, left, right and
centre, exuberantly Baroque and not at all Art Nouveau in their
details, and all the rest glass with the thinnest iron verticals
and horizontals.

    In France the architect with the keenest sense of the
potentialities of the new materials was Hector Guimard. It
was a fine show of a sense of topicality that the Paris Métro

94

93

95

allowed him for the relatively new purpose of a metropolitan
underpavement railway to design exclusively in the new
96.97
material. The general tenor is indeed as light as befits the
introduction to fast transport. But the details are bossy and
98
bony – more similar to Alfred Gilbert's of more than ten years
before than to anyone else's. However, the refusal to entertain
straight lines anywhere and the sense of inventiveness all
through place them firmly in Art Nouveau. Guimard's *magnum
opus*, the Castel Béranger of 1897–8, on the other hand is in its
façades not Art Nouveau. Its jumble of motifs is original, even

96, 97 OPPOSITE AND ABOVE The entrances designed by Hector Guimard for the Paris Métro are today probably the most insistent survivors from the age of Art Nouveau. Built between 1899 and 1904 they are still effective signposts

98 LEFT Guimard's ornament is as distinctive as Horta's. Detail of a Métro entrance by Guimard, a light in amber glass set in a strange organic budshape of green-finished cast iron
99 OPPOSITE Terracotta panels in the entrance to the Castel Béranger, Guimard's block of flats in Paris (1897–8); though the forms are still unmistakably 'Belle Epoque' they have no basis in nature

100–1 ABOVE AND OPPOSITE Two details from Guimard's Castel Béranger: (opposite) an eroded-looking seahorse shape of cast iron; and (above) the glass-brick wall of the staircase, set in an iron frame, foreshadowing long before Bruno Taut's Glass House (ill. 177) a favourite motif of the twenties and thirties

forcedly so, but it is angular, static, solid and conventional in many details. The ironwork of the main doors on the other hand and the terracotta panels in the entrance are Art

99
101 Nouveau and the latter are, moreover, most daring in their demonstration of pure abstraction. A rarely-seen iron detail from the top of the house reminds one of another architect who ventured into pure abstraction, Endell in his Elvira 'rocaille'.

89 In fact even some of the dragon connotations are the same. Yet more amazing historically is the wall of the staircase at the back, a wall of heavy double-curved glass panels of alternating

100 shapes whose very irregularity of surface does what in the terracotta panels had to be done by the craftsman's will.

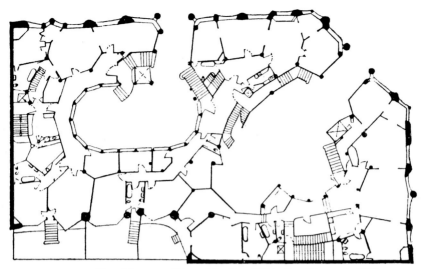

102 ABOVE Plan of the ground floor of the Casa Milá by Gaudí, begun in 1905.
This remained flexible till the last, with partition walls inserted only after the
building was complete
103 OPPOSITE Detail of the façade of Gaudí's Casa Milá, of dark, pitted stone –
deliberately wave-like, with seaweed balconies

Guimard's delight in materials and unexpected effects to
be obtained from them and even some of Guimard's forms
are the only causeway by which we can safely reach Gaudí.
There are few other communications, and his originality
might indeed not have become quite so extreme if it had not
been for his working in the comparative isolation of Barcelona
and working for a clientèle nationally disposed in favour of
fantastical architecture. Indeed the extremes of Plateresque
and Churrigueresque are hardly less bewildering than those of
Gaudí. These he must have known, but they do not seem to have
inspired him. On the other hand he must have been impressed
by the Mohammedan style of southern Spain as well as that
of folk building in Morocco. And he must also have seen in the
journals how Art Nouveau triumphed in France, and some of
the interior details in his two blocks of flats, the Casa Batlló
and the Casa Milá, are indeed entirely French Art Nouveau, just
as the use of concrete trees – leafless of course – in the Güell
Park is a conceit of Hennebique's, the French concrete fanatic.
Still, his overwhelming originality remains, but – at least in the
Casa Batlló and the Casa Milá, both late works, begun in 1905 –
it is an originality within the framework of Art Nouveau.

What after all is it that startles one in these façades as one
comes upon them unprepared in the Paseo de Gracia? A whole

102
103
104

façade in a slow, sluggish and somewhat menacing flow – like lava, some people have said; as if carved out by the sea, say others; like the face of a long-disused quarry, yet others. So here is undulation, and here is the affinity with nature 'structurized', as Van de Velde once called it. Here also – and this needs saying now at last – is that disregard for functional advantages that did such disservice to Art Nouveau in buildings and furnishings everywhere. Balcony railings which stab at you and consistently curved walls against which no one's furniture will stand satisfactorily are only two examples. What elevates these two late Gaudí buildings above those of other architects of the same moment is their restless force, their sense of masses in motion and their single-mindedness. The plan of the Casa Milá to which reference has already been made is ultimate proof that Art Nouveau principles could be applied to space as well as line and volume.

102

The placing of Gaudí within European Art Nouveau is relatively easy as long as one confines oneself to his work after 1903. But three years earlier he had started on the Güell Park and five years earlier on the chapel of Santa Coloma de Cervelló on an industrial estate also belonging to his patron Eusebio Güell. In the chapel there are no undulating lines; all is sharp, angular, aggressive. But all is also in its own idiom as unexpected as the houses in the Paseo de Gracia. If one looks for comparisons one is reminded rather of German Expressionism of the 1920s – in its wildest Dr Caligari dreams – than of Art Nouveau. As far as Art Nouveau was opposition to the past and opposition to the order of right-angles, Santa Coloma of course qualifies. As far as Art Nouveau was a challenging show of individualism, it also qualifies. And that is perhaps enough. The little building, abandoned before it was completed, is in its interpenetration of outer and inner spaces bolder than anything Frank Lloyd Wright had done or was ever to do in pursuit of spatial confluence. The walls are a seemingly arbitrary zigzag, though an axiality from entrance to altar is preserved. But the approach is wholly asymmetrical, and even the round piers inside do not correspond left with right. Moreover, supports are set at raking angles, they are built up here of brick, there of stones; they are roughly shaped or frankly shapeless, and they carry ribs whose details seem to have been decided not at the office, beforehand, but on the spot, as work went on.

86, 107

This is indeed true of the very similar structures connected with the Güell Park as well. Here also you find twisted supports

104 OPPOSITE At the Casa Batlló (1905–7) Gaudi refaced an older building with coloured tiles, adding the rippling stone entrance and bay-windows and spiky, sinister iron balconies, and finishing with a steep roof of tiles grading from orange to blue-green

105 In the crypt of Santa Coloma de Cervelló, begun in 1898, Gaudí's delight in variety of planes, textures and materials is obvious; his engineering instinct led him to the structurally efficient angles of walls and supports. He also designed the benches (see ill. 84)

106, 107 OPPOSITE AND RIGHT The transept front of Gaudí's Sagrada Familia was begun about 1887 in a free paraphrase of Gothic, and ended, in the twenties, in fantastic cubist pinnacles (right)

86

107

106
107

set diagonally, fairly normal but leaning Doric columns, stalactite vaults, quite apart from the dead trees of concrete, and quite apart from the enchanting back of the long seat running all along the open space at the top where nannies sit and children play. This back, writhing and drooping like a serpent or some antediluvian monster, is yet gay, by virtue of its delicious colours, bright, happy colours, any number of them and in haphazard relations. The seat is faced with faience and tiles, and here as well as on the roofs of his houses and indeed on the pinnacles of his great church, the Sagrada Familia, broken cups and saucers, broken floor tiles and wall tiles and chips of all kinds are used. Again Gaudí is closer to Picasso there than to the other practitioners of Art Nouveau.

The Sagrada Familia spans Gaudí's whole life. He dedicated his powers more and more to it and in the end to the exclusion of anything else. For Gaudí was an unquestioning Catholic. Religion was the centre of his life, and the aestheticism of much of Art Nouveau experimenting is totally absent in him. In 1884 he was put in charge of a neo-Gothic building only just begun.

108 ABOVE Gaudí's Palau Güell (1844–9), two arches with massive ironwork in the
Catalan tradition. Gaudí used parabolic arches – the shape of the future – both
decoratively and structurally
109 OPPOSITE Entrance to the Güell Park, begun in 1900. The stairs, flanked by
pavilions, surrounded a serpent fountain; they lead to the Market Hall with its
Doric colonnade

He continued it in that style and gradually turned freer and
bolder. As one looks at the great façade of the south transept,
one can watch the process of liberation. Below there are still
three tall gabled portals on the French Gothic cathedral pattern,
and it is only the decoration encrusting it that is transformed
into rockery and naturalistic leaf-work. The towers are without
precedent, but they were only started in 1903. And as for the
pinnacles, once again, it seems impossible to believe that they
can be the work of craftsmen working from architect's drawings.

107

Gaudí was not an architect in the sense in which the
profession had established itself in the nineteenth century and
was going to be run in the twentieth. He was not a professional
man working in an office. He was essentially still the medieval
craftsman whose final decision could only be taken as he
watched over the execution of what he had perhaps sketched
out on paper but never made final. In him one ideal of William
Morris had come true. What he built was 'by the people for
the people' and no doubt 'a joy for the maker', i.e., the actual
mason, as well.

It is of importance to say this; for recently Gaudí has
been hailed as a pioneer of twentieth-century structure,

a forerunner of Nervi. But whereas, in the field of new shapes and materials he points forward indeed, his use of complicated models to experiment with strains and stresses is not that of the engineer-architect of our age at all. On the contrary, it is still that of the individualist-craftsman, the outsider, the lonely, do-it-yourself inventor.

And in this extreme individualism once again Gaudí was part of Art Nouveau. For Art Nouveau was an outbreak of individualism first and foremost. It depended for success entirely on the personal force and sensibility of a designer or craftsman. What could be communicated of it, is what ruined it so quickly. The style of Schinkel, the style of Semper, the style of Pearson, the style of the Ecole des Beaux-Arts could be taught and used with impunity by the rank and file. Commercialized Van de Velde and Tiffany is a disaster. Commercialized Gaudí was hardly attempted. This individualism ties Art Nouveau to the century at whose end it stands. So does its insistence on craft and its antipathy against industry. So finally does its delight in the precious or at least the telling material.

But Art Nouveau straddles the boundary line between the two centuries, and its historical significance lies in those of its innovations which pointed forward. They are, as has been said in these pages more than once, its refusal to continue with the historicism of the nineteenth century, its courage in trusting its own inventiveness, and its concern with objects for use rather than with paintings and statues.

110 In Britain a style of chaste straight lines rivalled and indeed took the place of the sensuous curves of Continental Art Nouveau. This desk by Mackmurdo dates from 1886

Chapter 3
New Impetus from England

It is in its concern with objects for use that Art Nouveau was most decisively inspired by England. The message of William Morris was heeded everywhere. In other ways the relations between the English and the Continental developments of the 1890s are more complex. They deserve more than one close look. The situation, it must be remembered, was that in the 1880s Morris's art of design had reached its richest, most balanced maturity. A synthesis between nature and stylization was achieved which has never been outdone. At the same time in architecture Webb and Shaw had, at any rate in the field of domestic building, defeated Victorian pomposity and reintroduced a human scale and sensitive or at least telling details. And already before 1890 Morris as well as Shaw and Webb had their successors. The Arts and Crafts Exhibition Society had started and the progressive architectural journals had begun to illustrate the designs of Voysey, of Ernest Newton, Ricardo and others. Meanwhile, however, this Arts and Crafts movement had also benefited from those among the young who wanted to go beyond the enlightened traditionalism of Morris and Shaw. Mackmurdo, as we have seen, was their leader, and Mackmurdo with his Wren title-page of 1883 had started Art Nouveau. The effect of the journal of his Century Guild, the *Hobby Horse*, had been great, and English book art right on to Beardsley was indebted to it. But where Continental Art Nouveau of the 1890s acknowledged this debt freely and developed its own national versions out of English precedent, England itself turned away from it and followed Morris and Shaw rather than Art Nouveau.

Indeed, and this is perhaps the most surprising aspect of Mackmurdo's situation, he himself, when it came to designing buildings and furniture, did not apply the sinuosity of his

28
31

111 In this chair, designed in the early eighties, Mackmurdo used a traditional shape but with the swirling plant forms of his influential title-page (see ill. 28)

112 By 1886 Mackmurdo had moved on to the equally revolutionary angularity of the Century Guild exhibition stand: its thin vertical posts and 'mortar-board' tops were soon taken up – *via* Voysey and Mackintosh – as far away as Austria and Sweden

bookwork and textiles. The early chair which some regard – without sufficient evidence – as designed in 1881[53] has, apart from ornament directly connected with that of the Wren title-page, at least a curvaceous back, but the little desk of 1886 and the exhibition stand at Liverpool of the same year are entirely rational and rectangular. It is true they are in their own way as original as the proto-Art Nouveau of a few years before, but their originality is their slender square posts and the curious far-projecting hats or pieces of cornice each of them carries.

This motif in particular influenced Voysey and Mackintosh in their beginnings, and Voysey was also strongly influenced by Mackmurdo in his early textile designs. Charles F. Annesley Voysey must be regarded as the central figure in English architecture and design during the two decades around 1900. His style of domestic architecture was complete by 1890. In 1891 he built a small studio house in West Kensington, London, and there already

113 ABOVE Studio in West Kensington, London, by Voysey (1891), an exercise in rational design devoid of ornament. Note the pebbledash rendering, broad eaves and sloping buttresses – all Voysey trademarks
114, 115 OPPOSOTE Voysey specialized in country houses; Broadleys on Lake Windermere (opposite), of 1898, is remarkable for its plain bay windows with unmoulded mullions. The entrance of Vodin House, Pyrford Common, Surrey, of 1902 (opposite below), carries this simplicity even further

are the low, comfortable, spreading character, the bands of unmoulded window openings and of bare wall, the big, tapering chimneystacks. There is no longer even as much of period details as there had been in Shaw and Webb, but there remains all the same a strong period flavour, a flavour of the Tudor or Stuart cottage or manor house. The house is in its own way as original as Morris's designs, but hardly more original. In the late nineties and shortly after 1900 Voysey was extremely successful as a designer of private houses of moderate size, and for good reasons; for his plans are easy and at the same time his houses fit their setting, and their simple geometry was refreshing; they were eminently reasonable, unradical and unexacting.

Others in England at the same moment were bolder, none more so than E. S. Prior, W. R. Lethaby, and the much younger Edwin Lutyens. Prior, more distinguished as a scholar than as an architect, built a few houses between about 1895 and 1905 which combine Voysey's sixteenth- or seventeenth-century sympathy with a fanatical use of mixed local materials. Occasionally the bits of brick and the pebbles used in the raw are almost reminiscent of Gaudí. Lutyens was a man of brilliant talents who later turned away from the progressive developments and led the retreat into the grand manner which Shaw himself had started in his buildings after 1890. This neo-Baroque or neo-Classicism need not concern us here.

116 Home Place, Norfolk, by E. S. Prior (1904–6). Prior tried hard to revive local styles and local materials, preferring to be known as a 'builder' rather than an architect, but at Home Place his exotic mixture of flint, tile and brick takes him far from any true vernacular – almost into the realm of Gaudí

117 The early work of Edwin Lutyens has as much wit as Norman Shaw's and a prodigious architectural inventiveness. Tigbourne Court, Surrey (1897) is Lutyens at his best. Note the dramatic massing of the whole, the relation of the three gables to the excessively high chimney-stacks, and such details as the rusticated stonework with smooth banding

It reigned in official architecture nearly everywhere. Such public buildings as Nyrop's Town Hall at Copenhagen, begun in 1893, and Berlage's Exchange of Amsterdam of 1898 are highly exceptional in their free handling of traditional materials, and Nyrop at least stayed on safer ground even than Voysey. Of Lutyens' talents and his temptations into drama the finest show is Tigbourne Court of 1897.

118
119
117

118 ABOVE Interior of the Amsterdam Stock Exchange, 1898–1903. Berlage used
traditional red brick with stone dressings in a deliberately massive, angular style;
the vast iron roof is exposed and unornamented
119 OPPOSITE Copenhagen Town Hall by Martin Nyrop, 1892–1905. The façade and
spacious glazed courtyard still have many motifs from the Dutch sixteenth and early
seventeenth century, but they are handled as freely as Voysey handled his Tudor motifs

120 OPPOSITE Interior of All Saints, Brockhampton-by-Ross, Herefordshire, by W. R. Lethaby (1900–2). The tunnel-vault, of a shape more Expressionist than Gothic, is of concrete. With an ambivalence characteristic of the Arts and Crafts, it is thatched on the outside

121 RIGHT Clock designed by C. F. A. Voysey about 1906, of ebony with ivory inlay. The openwork crown is lined with yellow silk and topped by a brass ball like those it stands on

120

121

At least as dramatic, but without any of Lutyens' playfulness is the church designed by W. R. Lethaby at Brockhampton dating from 1900–2. Lethaby, after Morris the most constructive thinker on architecture and design in England, gave up practising altogether after Brockhampton in order to teach at the London Central School of Arts and Crafts which was the most progressive school of those years anywhere. Lethaby in his writings recommended the step from craft to industrial design, a step which Voysey and others already had taken as practising designers. But only Lethaby in England saw that more was concerned than a matter of production techniques.

122-4 An elegant simplicity of line characterized the best English products. Voysey designed silver as chaste as his houses – above right, a teapot of c. 1896 – and Ashbee was famous also on the Continent for such pieces as this silver dish (1899–1900, above left) with red-enamelled cover; its stone-set knob and ball feet are characteristic. Ernest Gimson designed beautifully-made inlaid furniture: his cabinet and stand of c. 1902 (opposite), like the ball feet of Ashbee's dish, derives ultimately from the seventeenth century

A style for industrial design was visualized by Lethaby but it was developed in practice in other countries. As far as the style is concerned, it mattered little whether what Voysey designed was in the end made by the craftsman or the manufacturer. The style is moderate, sensible, always graceful, whether in furniture or in textiles or in metalwork.

123

The same applies to other architects, designers and craftsmen. A chair such as that made by Baillie Scott for the Grand Duke of Hesse in 1898 is a good example, also in the design of the covering of the back which has abandoned the Art Nouveau way of Mackmurdo while keeping the sense of the pretty flat pattern. Another example is the exquisite cabinets designed by Ernest Gimson. They also are in no demonstrative way novel, yet in no way imitative, and they are a triumph of revived craftsmanship. However, the cabinet illustrated dates

122

from 1908, and by then, on the Continent, had lost all topicality. Gimson was trained as an architect and designed a few houses before he turned entirely to the crafts. The combination is characteristic of Britain at that moment. On the Continent, in terms of Art Nouveau, it was the painters rather who listened to

New Impetus from England

Morris. In Britain the message could be heard by the architects, because already at the Webb-Shaw stage the alliance with the Morris Movement had been established. One of the more interesting cases is that of C. R. Ashbee who designed houses of considerable originality, though obviously inspired by Shaw, and founded a Guild and School of Handicraft having learned the Morris lesson. The school operated at first in the East End of London, later at Chipping Campden in the Cotswolds; for Ashbee was keenly interested in social reform too. It is worth comparing the work of his craftsmen about 1900 with Continental work at the Paris Exhibition. What appears is that in furniture and metalwork for use Ashbee was entirely on the Voysey side, but in jewelry he comes remarkably close to Art Nouveau – a typically English compromise.

124

There was no compromise across the border in Scotland, where, suddenly, at the beginning of the 1890s, a group of architect-designers sprang up converting what they knew of Voysey and others in England and of work on the Continent too (for *The Studio* kept readers up-to-date) into an idiom entirely their own, as original and as radical as Art Nouveau, but never so contorted. Or at least not when they had reached maturity. The leader of the group was Charles Rennie Mackintosh, eleven years younger than Voysey, seventeen years younger than Mackmurdo. In addition there were his wife and her sister – the sisters Macdonald – his brother-in-law McNair, and a few others. The diploma document of Mackintosh, datable to 1893, is contorted indeed. The nearest parallel to these lean, sombre nudes is Toorop in Holland, and their completely abstract bands of hair, their draperies and trees reduced to one leaf (or fruit) on each upward growing branch are entirely Mackintosh's. In the next few years they did other stationery, and the ladies did repoussé work as well. Then Mackintosh's great opportunity came. In 1896 he won the competition for a new building for the Glasgow School of Art, and the building was erected in 1897–1909. In 1897 *The Studio* published an illustrated article on the group. In 1900 they exhibited in Vienna, in 1902 in Turin. In 1901 Mackintosh went in for a competition set by a German publisher – designing a house for a lover of art. Glasgow was in fact destined to find more resonance on the Continent than in England.

125 OPPOSITE Charles Rennie Mackintosh, washstand, 1904

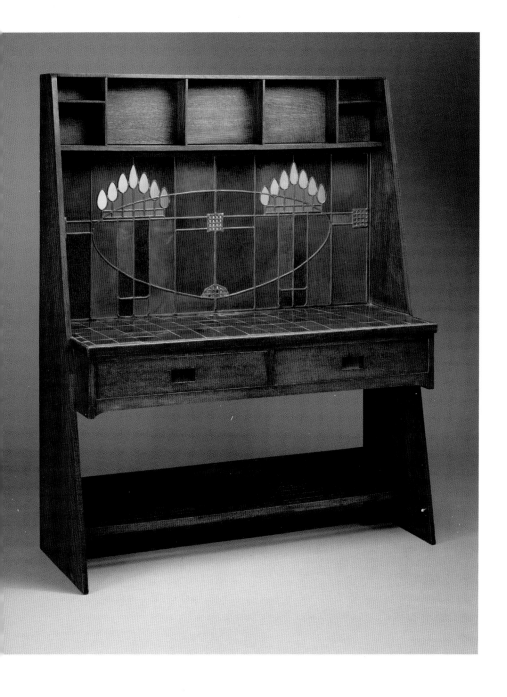

126 BELOW Mackintosh designed this diploma for the Glasgow School of Art Club in 1893 – the year in which Toorop's *The Three Brides* appeared in *The Studio*. The influence is obvious, but Mackintosh's sparseness and angularity are already unmistakable. Note too the compressed lettering

127 OPPOSITE Mirror-frame of pure beaten tin by Mackintosh's wife Margaret and her sister Frances Macdonald. It takes its title, *Honesty*, and its pattern from a plant; the bodies of the women at either side are reduced to elongated abstract shapes (*c*. 1896; 70 cm, 29 ins. wide)

The front of the Glasgow School of Art sets the theme for all that Mackintosh was to do in the next ten or twelve years. Between 1900 and 1911 he had plenty of work at Glasgow, a number of private houses, a number of tea-rooms, a school, and some interior work. England however remained closed to him, and from about 1910 his star waned. He was a fascinating but a difficult, erratic man, and he alienated clients' sympathies in the dour city of Glasgow. For the last fifteen years of his life he had hardly any commissions.

The front of the School of Art is primarily a wall of large studio windows facing north. They have the English Tudor motif of mullions and transoms, but the mullions and transoms are, like those of Voysey, completely unmoulded. The front would be a functional grid, if it were not for the entrance bay or frontispiece which is placed out of the centre and is a free, asymmetrical composition of elements of the Baroque, of the Scottish baronial past and of the Shaw-Voysey tradition. The pediment on the first floor belongs to the first, the bare turret to the second, the little oriel windows to the third. Moreover, the functional grid and the sturdiness of the centre are relieved by delightful, very thin metalwork, the area railings, the handrail of the balcony and especially the odd hooks carrying transparent, flower-like balls in front of the upper windows. Their practical purpose is to hold boards for window-cleaning, but their aesthetic purpose, like that of all the other metalwork is to provide a delicate screen of light and playful forms through which the stronger and sounder rest will be seen. Inside the building too there are transparent screens of slender wooden posts, sudden surprises of relations between forms, especially in the boardroom, where pilasters are treated as an abstract grid of a Mondrian kind below their perfectly harmless Ionic capitals, and on the roof, where shapes are almost as bold and abstract as Gaudí's and Le Corbusier's at Ronchamp, and there are again the most unexpected curligigs of metal.

Once more only did Mackintosh design a building as functional as the School of Art – the Concert Hall for the Glasgow Exhibition of 1901, designed in 1898. It was to be circular and to hold over four thousand people. Mackintosh provided for a low building with a saucer dome on mighty buttresses. The supports were of iron, forming a span of about 50 metres (165 ft). The organ, the artists' rooms and services were in an attachment with polygonal walls and curved parapets and roof. The design gained no prize.

While the building was severely plain, the organ-case would have had all the finesses and surprises of Mackintosh's

128

130

131

133

128 Entrance of the Glasgow School of Art, 1897–9, by Mackintosh. Above the door is the window of the Director's study, and above that his studio. The main studios have vast iron-framed windows

129 ABOVE Entrance lobby of the Glasgow
School of Art, 1897–9. Mackintosh used bold
forms covered with smooth cement, with
small tile or metalwork inserts
130 OPPOSITE Paraphrase of an Ionic pilaster
in the board room of the Glasgow School of
Art (1907–9)

131-3 BELOW AND OPPOSITE Mackintosh's keen and completely modern sculptural sense appears (below) in a wrought-iron lamp bracket over the stairs in the Glasgow School of Art (1897–9), (opposite above) in the bold roughcast forms of an arch on the roof of the School of Art (c. 1907), and (opposite below) in his revolutionary and unrewarded design of 1898 for a circular concert hall with projecting dressing-rooms etc.

134-7 Mackintosh's furniture has the same sureness and originality as his architecture. Left, a bedroom chair with back of flower-stencilled canvas, and below left, a table inlaid with ivory – both of c. 1900 and enamelled white, a fashion Mackintosh created. Opposite, two chairs of 1902 for a bedroom in Hill House, with Mackintosh's characteristic ladder slats going right down to the floor; and below right, a table for the same house, of ebonized wood but with mother-of-pearl inlay, that carries geometrical intricacy even further

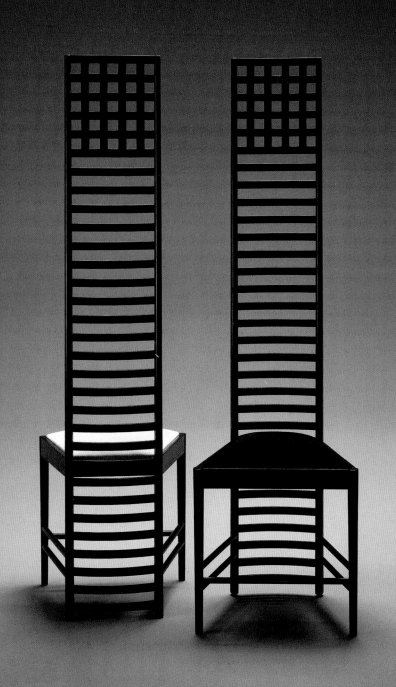

furniture design. What characterizes all Mackintosh furniture can be said to be a successful synthesis of the contrasting criteria of England and the Continent. Take, for example the two tables illustrated. One is as square as a Voysey and indeed more rigidly so – as close in its grid as a cage – the second is oval, with two small oval set-in rose and ivory panels of abstract curves. Moreover, the first table has a black finish, the second a glossy white one, and white and rose, white and lilac, with black, and perhaps silver and mother-of-pearl became Mackintosh's favourite colours. These sophisticated, precious colours harmonize to perfection with the sophistication of his slender uprights and shallow curves. But the radicalism of ornamental abstraction and the lyrical softness of the colours also contradict each other, and it is the tension between the sensuous and the structural elements that makes Mackintosh's decoration unique. But as one looks at some of the most remarkable chairs by Mackintosh, one's conviction might well be shaken that his use of grids is indeed structural – in the sense of the skyscraper grids. The hard verticals and horizontals must have been an attraction to Mackintosh in themselves, an aesthetic counterpoint to his tense curves, and a safeguard that the frail blooms and feminine hues do not cloy.

Mackintosh's fame was greater on the Continent than in Britain, let alone in England. The exhibition of 1900 in Vienna, the competition of 1901 in Germany where he was placed second – Baillie Scott won first prize – and the exhibition of 1902 in Turin have already been mentioned. What made it possible for the Continent to admire him was precisely what deprived him of patronage in England. He was too Art Nouveau, and England, after the few years of her Art Nouveau *avant la lettre* had, as we have seen, turned away from everything *outré*. Indeed, when in 1900 some mostly French Art Nouveau furniture had been acquired from the Paris exhibition by a private donation for the Victoria and Albert Museum, protests were published in the press – one of them signed by E. S. Prior, saying that 'this work is neither right in principle nor does it evince a proper regard for the material employed'.[54] Those who protested were of course right within their own terms of reference. They were also right from the point of view of the arising twentieth century. Art Nouveau can only be appreciated on purely aesthetic grounds – and its products might well be called unprincipled. But if these are looked at on aesthetic grounds, as they were in Austria and Germany, what a find the Glasgow group was. Vienna was particularly responsive, because Vienna in 1900

138 Joseph Olbrich's exhibition hall for the Secession in Vienna, of 1898: a clean massing of geometrical shapes. The 'dome' of metal leaves is echoed, in Olbrich's original drawing, by two equally round laurel bushes flanking the door

138

was, on her own, already on the way to a straightening out of the Art Nouveau fancies. Joseph Olbrich's building of 1898 for the Secession, the club of young artists in opposition, proves that. While it has a wrought-iron dome the intertwined laurel-branches of which are Art Nouveau, the dome also is a pure hemisphere, and the walls are sheer. What the same Secession then showed of Mackintosh's work was a confirmation and made converts – none more successful than Josef Hoffmann. *Quadratl*-Hoffmann became his nickname,

139

because of his preference for squares and rectangles in his decoration. Olbrich was called to Darmstadt by the Grand Duke of Hesse in 1899. The Grand Duke, a grandson of Queen Victoria, commissioned furniture and interior decoration for his palace from Ashbee and Baillie Scott. The German publishing house which had set the competition for the house of an art lover and which published Mackintosh's design was also in Darmstadt. Looking at Mackintosh's designs one can

140

understand why he took Germany and Austria by storm. Here

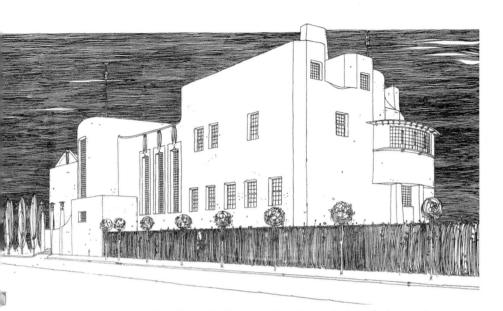

139 OPPOSITE Josef Hoffmann, like his master Otto Wagner, believed in the complete unity of architecture, décor and furnishings; a rectilinear interior designed c. 1900
140 ABOVE Competition design by Mackintosh for a 'house for an artlover', published in Germany in 1901 and highly influential

was the wilfulness and irregularity of Art Nouveau handled with an exquisite finesse previously unknown. But here was also a sense of slender, erect verticals and smooth, unbroken surfaces which might well serve as a weapon to defeat Art Nouveau. Adherents of Art Nouveau and its just-emerging opponents could replenish their arsenals from the *Haus eines Kunstfreundes*.

The ubiquity and intensity of British influence on the Continent during these years is evident. Its conflicting directions, however, require some comment. The influence started with Morris and the Domestic Revival. It stood then for a revived interest in craft, that is, the provision of objects for use, and for an appreciation of the modest, comfortable, middle-class house as against the pomposity of the public building and the rich man's villa. Then came the influence of Morris's Kelmscott Press on the one hand – which meant again a sense of aesthetic responsibility, this time in the art of the book – and of Mackmurdo and ultimately Beardsley on the other, and this encouraged Art Nouveau rather than responsibility. Voysey again stood for reason, domestic comfort and prettiness in the design of interior furnishings; Ashbee and Baillie Scott a little more floridly for the same. Mackintosh alone, to repeat, could be a witness for the defence and for the prosecution of both Art Nouveau and anti-Art Nouveau. Olbrich in 1901[55] defended Art Nouveau against England: 'It is only if one can feel both democratically and autocratically, that one can evaluate the imaginative craftsman who wants to express in decorative art more than mere utility. One may then even approach the question which no one now ventures to touch: which forces are more valuable for a nation, those which evolve rationally, consciously and intellectually good forms ... or those which create in the abundant plenitude of their inventiveness hundreds of new shapes and visions, each carrying the germs of new possibilities... The limit to which one may advance in expressiveness without getting aesthetically objectionable becomes confused ... must lie at different levels for different natures and must affect different natures differently... Just as it is not given to the Englishman to utter the wealth of emotion expressed by the German soul in the untold variety of its music, the English spirit cannot ornamentally and constructively express itself with force, violence, agitation, fantasy.' But others, several years earlier, already praised England for these very limitations. This is what Edmond de Goncourt meant in 1896 when he called the new style Yachting Style. This is why, in the same year, *Pan*, the lavish only just established journal for modern art and decoration in Germany, brought out an article on English Art in the House, and this is what made Adolf Loos say that 'the centre of European civilization is at present in London'[56] and what made the Prussian Board of Trade send Hermann Muthesius to England to stay there for several years and study English architecture and design.

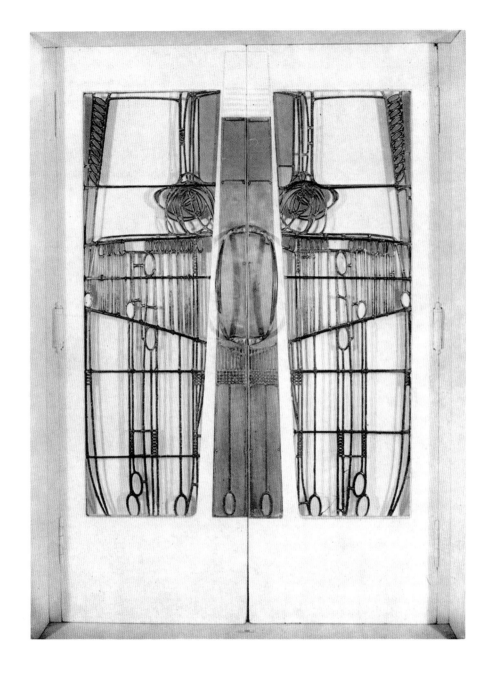

141 Doors by Mackintosh for the Willow Tea Rooms, 1904. Using glass of his favourite pastel colours set in lead and steel panels on white wood, he creates an abstract pattern of nervous yet muted excitement

142 Central span of the Garabit railway viaduct by Gustave Eiffel: an arch-bridge of iron, 120 metres (400 ft) above the river. Eiffel had already used the same system in 1877 in his design for the Maria Pia Bridge in Portugal

Chapter 4
Art and Industry

Vienna was first on the Continent in returning to the straight
path of the straight line and the square and rectangle, and,
being Vienna, succeeded in preserving the elegance and
the sense of precious materials of Art Nouveau. In Germany
the change is principally connected with the names of
Riemerschmid and Peter Behrens, and while the change in
Austria was an aesthetic one entirely, in Germany it was also
social. Riemerschmid and his brother-in-law, Karl Schmidt,
the founder of the *Deutsche Werkstätten*, as early as 1899
began to tackle the problem of cheap furniture and in 1905
at an exhibition showed their first machine-made furniture,
173   designed, they said, 'from the spirit of the machine'. Behrens,
who had belonged to the colony of artists at Darmstadt,
abandoned the curve about 1904 and turned to cubic shapes
and square decoration, as they had done in Vienna, but
with greater severity. A few years later he was given the
opportunity by the A.E.G., the German electricity combine,
of concentrating for a time entirely on factory architecture
169   and industrial design. But already in 1898 he had designed
glass for quantity production.

In France the revolt against Art Nouveau took yet another
form. It centred on the conquest of the new materials by new
architects. The triumphs of iron architecture at the exhibition
of 1889 had still been the triumphs of engineers, even if the
Eiffel Tower by its very height and position became at once
one of the chief constituents of the architectural scene of
Paris. Being a monument and not a work of utility such as
the grandest of the exhibition halls and bridges – Eiffel's own
142   Garabit Viaduct of 1880–8 with a span of 165 metres (543 ft),
the two Roeblings' Brooklyn Bridge of 1867–83 with a span of
144   485 metres (1,595 ft), Fowler and Baker's Firth of Forth Bridge

143-4 OPPOSITE AND ABOVE Eiffel's tower for the Paris Exhibition of 1889, a virtuoso display of ironwork 300 metres (984 ft) high; (above) the Firth of Forth Bridge by Fowler and Baker, 1881–7, the most splendid of all cantilever bridges

143

of 1881–7 with a span of 520 metres (1,710 ft), the first an arch bridge, the second a suspension bridge, the third a cantilever bridge – the Eiffel Tower had more chance to be looked at by layman and architect alike as a piece of design with aesthetic connotations, that is, as architecture. Indeed Muthesius, the Prussian architect whose studies in England have been mentioned, listed in a book of 1902, called characteristically *Stilarchitektur und Baukunst*, the Crystal Palace, the Bibliothèque Ste-Geneviève, the Halle des Machines and the Eiffel Tower as examples of the right kind of architecture for the twentieth century. In 1913 he added to his list train-sheds and grain elevators.[57]

Train-sheds were of iron and glass, but grain elevators were of concrete. France had led the world in the aesthetic appreciation of iron – the part played by Labrouste and Viollet-le-Duc has been discussed – she was now going to lead in that of concrete. The first concrete fanatic of many was François Coignet. He wrote at the time of the exhibition of 1855 that 'cement, concrete and iron' would replace stone, and the year after took a patent for iron members embedded in concrete – not the first such patent incidentally – in which they are called *tirants*, showing that the tensile strength of mass concrete was appreciated. In the seventies Joseph Monier worked on posts and beams of reinforced concrete, and Americans and Germans made the necessary analyses and calculations on the performance of the two materials in conjunction. Finally, in the nineties François Hennebique built factories of concrete with steel reinforcements on the utilitarian grid principle. The factory illustrated here is of 1895. In 1894 already Anatole de Baudot, a pupil first of Labrouste, then of Viollet-le-Duc, and their true follower in the sense that he followed their principles rather than their forms, decided to use concrete for his church of St-Jean de Montmartre and not to conceal it. There are pointed as well as round arches and rib vaults. The internal character is Gothic, the exterior only vestigially medieval.

147

145-6

145-6 OPPOSITE AND ABOVE Anatole de Baudot, in St-Jean de Montmartre (1894–1902) was the first to use reinforced concrete systematically in a non-industrial building. It is combined with brick in the façade. The interior has rib-vaults and other reminiscences of the Gothic past

While Baudot's church was still incomplete, in 1902 Auguste
148 Perret, thirty years younger, designed the celebrated house in
150 the rue Franklin. It has many titles to fame. It is the first
private house to use concrete framing. It demonstrates this
fact proudly; even if the concrete posts and beams are still
clad in terracotta, it distinguishes with care between the
appearance of supporting members and infilling panels –
the latter are in lively Art Nouveau leaf patterns of faience –
it opens the façade in a U-shape to avoid a backyard, and it

147 OPPOSITE One of the first buildings to use reinforced concrete throughout, allowing vast windows: François Hennebique's spinning mill at Tourcoing, of 1895
148 ABOVE The first domestic use of a concrete skeleton: Auguste Perret's block of flats in Paris, 25bis rue Franklin (1902). Perret devised a U-shaped plan to allow as much window surface as possible

faces its staircase entirely with glass hexagons, proclaiming in this its indebtedness to Guimard's Castel Béranger. In 1905 in his garage in the rue de Ponthieu Perret exposed his concrete skeletons naked; in 1911 in the Théâtre des Champs-Elysées he introduced the concrete skeleton into public architecture. To the end, however, he refused to test concrete for its possibilities of wide cantilevers and curved surfaces in tension. This was left to others, one French by nation, the other at least by race and name.

149

149 BELOW The Théâtre des Champs-Elysées in Paris (1911) by Perret is one of the earliest monumental buildings constructed entirely with a reinforced concrete frame. In this drawing the frame is shown: the stage is at the right, and the gallery tiers appear in section
150 OPPOSITE In Perret's rue Franklin flats the angular outline and projecting bays are determined by the concrete frame, but this is hidden behind terracotta and Art Nouveau tiles

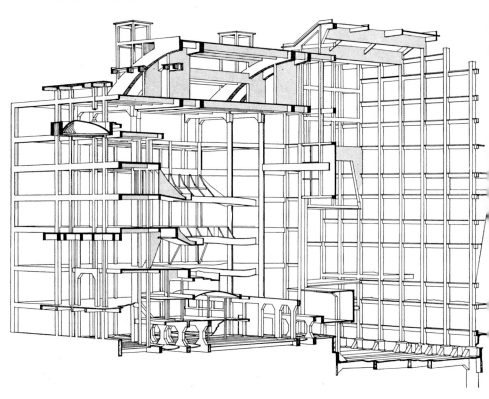

151 Tony Garnier's plan for a vast Industrial City, developed in 1899–1904 though not finished until 1917, was revolutionary in its scope and its use of reinforced concrete throughout. It was planned around the needs of factories and communications – foreground, the railway yards and docks – with simple, convenient housing for the workers. A dam (in the distance) would provide power.

152 Houses in Garnier's *Cité Industrielle*: simple cubic shapes of concrete, surrounded by public gardens

Tony Garnier was a few years older than Perret. He won the Prix de Rome in 1899, but used most of his time there to develop the plan and the architecture of an ideal industrial town. The result was sent to the academy in 1901, but at first refused. It was exhibited in 1904 and published – not without revisions – in 1917. Meanwhile, in 1905 Edouard Herriot, a socialist like Garnier, and at the time mayor of Lyons, had begun to make use of Garnier for municipal building. This gave him the opportunity to realize some of his ideas. What makes the *Cité Industrielle* a milestone in the history of the early twentieth century is that here for the first time a young architect took as his theme the needs of a town of today; 'for industrial requirements', he stated in the introduction, 'will be responsible for the foundation of most new towns in the future'. The plan is developed on a possible site, somewhere, Garnier says, in the south-east of France, his own homeland. The town is to have thirty-five thousand inhabitants. The plan refuses to have anything to do with academic tenets of axiality but aims to work in the interests of those who would live and work in the

153 Railway station of the *Cité Industrielle*, with large windows, a bold concrete tower and even bolder cantilevered roofs. This, however, was designed shortly before 1917, not in 1904[58]

town. Planners sixty years later may raise their objections; the plan yet remains pioneer work. The houses have no backyards. Each house has at least one bedroom window to the south. The built-over area does not exceed half the plot. The rest is public green-spaces. There are plenty of pedestrian passages. The materials used are cement for foundations, reinforced concrete for beams and ceilings. 'All the major buildings are constructed almost exclusively in reinforced concrete.' This one sees at once; the cantilevered roofs of the Municipal Offices and station would be impossible otherwise and go far beyond what had at the time been executed. The cubic shapes of the small houses were as revolutionary. Decoration is not banished but remains 'completely independent of the construction'. Garnier never had an opportunity to realize anything as bold and sweeping as the *Cité Industrielle*, but in the Public Slaughterhouse at Lyons, built in 1906–13, he did demonstrate dignity in industrial architecture, and he was one of the very few anywhere in the world to do so. We shall return presently to success in this field in Germany. But first the story of reinforced concrete must be

152

153

154

Art and Industry

rounded off by reference to the discovery of the new combined material's structural and aesthetic advantages in the field of arcuated as well as trabeated architecture. Here the first in the field was once more an engineer: Robert Maillart, a Swiss, but a pupil of Hennebique. He first suggested and carried out improvements on the current system of warehouse or factory construction with posts and beams of concrete by making one the formerly supporting and supported parts. The mushroom principle he evolved was discovered at the same time in America. Soon after, he turned to bridges and again succeeded in making the arch and the roadway one. In France at the same moment, to be precise in 1910, Simon Boussiron, another engineer, built the roof of the railway station of Bercy near Paris

156

155

154 BELOW The closest Garnier came to building his Industrial City: part of the vast slaughterhouse of La Mouche, Lyons, 1909–13. It includes a cattle market. The buildings are of concrete, but the vault of the market hall (span about 80 metres, 265 ft) is of steel and glass
155 OPPOSITE ABOVE Goods stations at Bercy, outside Paris, by Simon Boussiron (1910): the roof is of thin shells of concrete, top-glazed, and concrete has allowed a daring cantilever at the side
156 OPPOSITE BELOW Reinforced concrete appeared in bridge-building with Robert Maillart's bridge over the Rhine at Tavanesa (Switzerland) of 1910. Arch and roadway are a single unit, aesthetically as well as structurally. The influence of Maillart began to be felt only after the Second World War

157-8 Max Berg's Centenary Hall, Breslau, of 1913, fully exploited the possibilities of concrete. It covers an area of 21,000 square feet with an economy and grandeur hardly equalled until Nervi. Opposite, a detail of the reinforced concrete ribs

of very thin concrete vaults of the hyperbolic parabaloid shape the future of which was to be so spectacular.[59] But the aesthetic possibilities of arches combining the long sweep of steel with the solidity of stone in architecture, acknowledged by the public as such, were first recognized to the full by Max Berg in his

157-8 Centenary Hall of 1913 at Breslau. Max Berg is not as well known as he deserves to be. This is largely due to the fact that already before 1925 he abandoned architecture to devote himself to a Christian mysticism. And who can say whether Lothar Schreyer of both *Sturm* and Bauhaus who tells us about this is so wrong in seeing even in the Centenary Hall 'the Cosmos opened to reveal the courses of the stars and the Empyraeum'.[60]

The famous names in the Germany and Austria of Perret's, Garnier's and Maillart's generation are Josef Hoffmann and Adolf Loos in Austria, Peter Behrens in Germany. To them must be added Otto Wagner, professor at the academy of art in Vienna, who was only seven years younger than Morris. In his inaugural lecture, in 1894, he reiterated Viollet-le-Duc's faith in the modern age, the need to find forms to express it,

159, 160 ABOVE AND LEFT Otto Wagner's early stations for the Vienna Stadtbahn display little interest in either modern forms or the new mode of transport they served

161 OPPOSITE While Wagner believed that architecture should reflect modern life in modern materials, only in 1905, in the glass and steel hall of the Vienna Postal Savings Bank, did he achieve his ideal

and the conviction that 'nothing that is not practical can be beautiful'.[61] His buildings of those years were less radical. His stations of the Stadtbahn of 1894–1901 are in a kind of Baroque Art Nouveau, emphatically less stimulating than Guimard's Métro which they preceeded, and his office buildings and flats are simple, but in their fenestration not untraditional. The favourite facing with faience reminds one of Perret. Only one of all Wagner's works has the prophetic character which we found for the first time in Garnier's *Cité Industrielle*: the interior of the Postal Savings Bank of 1905, with its tapering metal supports and its curved glass roof.

159

161

In speaking of prophetic character here, one is perhaps not quite right. The buildings of the *Cité Industrielle* and the Postal Savings Bank are not prophetic of the twentieth century: they belong to it, that is, they contributed to its creation, out of the new materials and their authentically integrated use, out of the anti-historicism of Art Nouveau and out of William Morris's faith in serving people's needs. The buildings designed in the same years by Josef Hoffmann and Adolf Loos must be looked at in the same way. Hoffmann's Palais Stoclet in Brussels

162-4 In 1905 Josef Hoffmann was commissioned to design a palatial house (above) for M. Stoclet in Brussels. The result proved that the new style, with its bare straight lines, was as suitable for gracious living as for commerce. Opposite above, the dining-room, with marble veneers and mosaics by Klimt (see ill. 166); opposite below, the hall, rising through two storeys

162-4

163
166

demonstrated once and for all that the new style with its reliance on unmitigated right angles was as suitable for luxury as for pure function, for leisure as for work. The secret, if you are bent on banishing ornament, mouldings, curves altogether, is fine materials and the play of proportions. The latter determines the varied and lively exterior of the Palais Stoclet, the former the interior with its marble facings and its large mosaics by Klimt. The mosaic is flat decoration, Klimt's scroll trees and figures are exquisitely flattened, and their perfect suitability to Hoffmann's ensemble shows once more the part Art Nouveau could play in the creation of the twentieth-century style.

165 ABOVE In revolt against what he considered the prettiness of fashionable Viennese architecture, Adolf Loos banished every suggestion of ornament and almost of charm. His Steiner House, Vienna (1910) shows him at his most uncompromising

166 OPPOSITE *The Fulfilment Group (Embrace)* (1905–6), by Gustav Klimt, water-colour and gouache design for a mosaic for the dining-room of Hoffmann's Palais Stoclet (ill. 162)

Adolf Loos hated Hoffmann and the Wiener Werkstätte of which Hoffmann was one of the founders and which succeeded in combining the new, post-Art Nouveau style with an inimitably Viennese daintiness and prettiness. For the initial patron of the Werkstätte, the man who had put the necessary money at the disposal of the founder, Mackintosh had designed a music room. Loos was the purist of the emerging movement. *Ornament and Crime* is the title of his most often quoted essay. This was published in 1908. The purest of his purist houses and therefore the most often illustrated is the Steiner House in Vienna of 1910. Here for the first time the layman would find it hard to decide whether this might not be of 1930.

165

The greatest contribution of Germany during these years
was the foundation of the Deutscher Werkbund in 1907, the
society in which architects, craftsmen and manufacturers
met and in which the new conception of industrial design was
evolved, a conception whose origin in England – in spite of
all the conflicts between Morris's faith in craft and the new
equally enthusiastic faith in the machine – is made patent
by the fact that the term *design* had in the end to be taken
over by Germany because of the absence of a German word
with the same meaning. An appreciation of the machine and
its possibilities was not in itself new, and a kind of aesthetic
worship of the machine can be found here and there in all
countries and in all decades of the nineteenth century. As
early as 1835 in a parliamentary enquiry in England into the
relation between qualities of design and Britain's exports the
neo-classical architect T. L. Donaldson had said that he knew
no 'example of a perfect machine which is not at the same time
beautiful'.[62] Redgrave, one of Henry Cole's circle, in his report
on design at the 1851 exhibition, had similarly written that in
objects 'where use is so paramount that ornament is repudiated
... a noble simplicity is the result'.[63] And so it goes on to
Oscar Wilde, the aesthete: 'All machinery may be beautiful...

Do not seek to decorate it.'[64] But it was still a far step from Wilde's purely aesthetic reaction and the Cole circle's recognition of the problem on paper, to its final facing and solving by the Werkbund.

The Werkbund published year-books in the years 1912–15, and they contain the record of what was achieved. Illustrated are a tea-set by Riemerschmid for the Deutsche Werkstätten, linoleum by Riemerschmid for the Delmenhorst Linoleum factory, and electric kettles and fans by Behrens for the A.E.G.

The case of Behrens is the most significant in Europe at that moment. The Allgemeine Elektrizitätsgellschaft or A.E.G. under its director Paul Jordan took up the new Werkbund principles in earnest and made Behrens the architect of their buildings, factories as well as shops, the designer of their products and even their stationery. Behrens was the first of the line that leads to the present-day American stylists or Gio Ponti and

168
167
172-4

174-5

167, 168 Designs by Richard Riemerschmid for mass production: (opposite) furnishing fabric, 1905, and (below) a tea-set for the Deutsche Werkstätten

169-73 Germany led the world in design for industry with the work of such men as Riemerschmid and Behrens. Above, glass bottles designed by Riemerschmid in 1912 and left, champagne glasses of 1899 by Behrens; opposite, electric kettle and fan for the A.E.G., 1912 and a chair of 1899 by Riemerschmid.

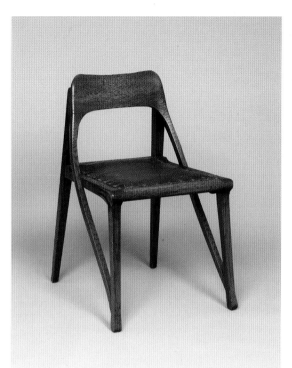

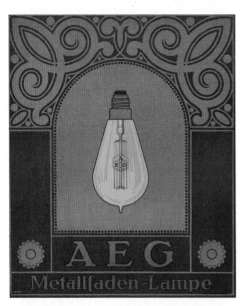

174-5 LEFT AND BELOW Peter Behrens was both architect and chief designer for A.E.G. He was responsible for everything from their posters (left) to their factory buildings in Berlin (below) of 1907
176 OPPOSITE The Fagus factory at Alfeld on the Leine, designed in 1910 by Behrens' young pupil Walter Gropius, summed up all that had been achieved in pre-war industrial architecture. Slim brick posts, and all the rest glass; no posts at the corners at all

Arne Jacobsen. But his buildings seen purely as architecture are as important. What Garnier was doing at Lyons, Behrens did in Berlin, and his expression of the nobility of work is even purer, and more detached from motifs of the past, than Garnier's.

The final synthesis of all that had been developed in industrial architecture to that time is the Fagus factory for shoe-trees at Alfeld on the Leine, which was designed by the much younger Walter Gropius, pupil of Behrens, in collaboration with Adolf Meyer, in 1910, the very year of Loos's Steiner House. The two buildings have this in common: a ruthlessly cubic shape and the total absence of ornament. But Gropius dealt with a novel job, Loos with an old one, and Gropius courageously picked up the threads of the existing, utilitarian, essentially anonymous architecture of glass set in a structural frame, such as they were to illustrate it in the Werkbund year-book of 1913. And he imbued it with the nobility he had seen in Behrens' factories and a social awareness ultimately derived from the Morris Movement.

The illustrations just referred to accompanied an article by Gropius on the development of modern industrial architecture in one of the Werkbund year-books. Other articles were by Riemerschmid, by Behrens and also by Muthesius, who more than any other was responsible for leading the Werkbund in the twentieth-century direction. He had to fight his case against the opposition of Van de Velde, who pleaded for individual expression where Muthesius wanted to develop standards.

Chapter 5
Towards the International Style

Muthesius in the famous discussion at Cologne in 1914 said: 'Architecture and with it the whole area of activity of the Werkbund moves towards standardization (*Typisierung*)... Only standardization can ... once again introduce a universally valid, self-certain taste.' Van de Velde answered: 'As long as there are artists in the Werkbund ... they are going to protest against any suggestion of a canon of standardization. The artist, according to his innermost essence, is a fervent individualist, a free, spontaneous creator. He will never voluntarily submit to a discipline forcing on him a type, a canon.' It must have been a memorable moment – Art Nouveau at its best resisting the needs and declining the responsibilities of the new century.

In fact the victory of Muthesius was assured even before the Cologne meeting. The meeting was held apropos the first Werkbund exhibition, and this exhibition, at least in its most important buildings, actually demonstrated that victory, and would have demonstrated it internationally if the outbreak of the First World War had not disrupted European unity and held up cultural progress. Among the buildings, Behrens's Festival Hall was disappointingly classical, Hoffmann's Austrian pavilion equally classical outside, but inside had a playfulness which was as backward-pointing, as was Van de Velde's impressive theatre with its emphatic curves. The two most powerful buildings were the Glass House by Bruno Taut and Gropius's *Halle des Machines* and attached offices of a fictitious factory. Taut's prismatic dome was the most original shape in the exhibition, a prophecy of geodesic domes to come. The glass wall below is in the line of descent of Guimard and Perret.

177
178

177 OPPOSITE Staircase in Bruno Taut's Glass House at the Cologne Werkbund Exhibition of 1914, entirely of glass bricks (cf. ill. 100) and iron

178 ABOVE Glass House by Bruno Taut (1914), with a prismatic dome
foreshadowing Buckminster Fuller
179 OPPOSITE Carson Pirie Scott store, Chicago, by Sullivan (1899–1924).
Note the dominant steel frame, clad in white terracotta and ending in a (since
removed) eaves gallery; the 'Chicago windows' (fixed centre and movable
sides); and the lush ornament framing the display windows (see ill. 26)

Gropius at this moment was clearly influenced, not only by
Behrens but even more by Frank Lloyd Wright whose work had
been made known to Europe first by two publications issued in
Berlin in 1910 and 1911 and then by lectures of Berlage's who had
himself visited Chicago in 1911.

179   The Chicago to which he made his pilgrimage was, however,
no longer that of Sullivan, though Sullivan was still alive.
After the completion of the Carson Pirie Scott store in 1904, he
received no further commissions of importance and died lonely
and disappointed in 1922. When at the great Chicago Exhibition
of 1893 the classicism of Beaux-Arts derivation had triumphed,
he had prophesied that this would put back architecture in
America by fifty years. He was nearly right. The so-called School
of Chicago fizzled out during the last years before the First
World War, and though something equally influential took
its place, it was not of the calibre of the work of the School of
Chicago. What had been work in new materials and for new
purposes was replaced by work – admittedly aesthetically
brilliant – in the limited field of the private house.

Towards the International Style

180-1 BELOW AND RIGHT Frank Lloyd Wright was in the office of Louis Sullivan when he produced the Charnley House, Chicago (1891–2, below), with Sullivanesque ornament on the balcony. It is still a closed design, but its low projecting roof and general severity hint at his later buildings such as the Martin House, Buffalo (right) of 1903–5, with its complex interpenetration of indoor and outdoor space

Yet Frank Lloyd Wright's is not entirely an aesthetic achievement. What it consisted of is easily said: a new vision of the house embedded in its natural surroundings and opening towards them by means of terraces and cantilevered 182 roofs, and a new vision of the interior of the house as freely intercommunicating spaces. There was practical precedent for both these things in American domestic building before him; as an aesthetic experience they belong to him entirely and by their influence from 1910 onwards they established new ideals for Europe as well. The operative dates are these: the Charnley 180 House of 1891, severely cubic but closed; the Winslow House of 1893 with far oversailing eaves but still closed; the Studio, Oak Park of 1895, the first with a complex interlocked plan, and so to the watershed of 1900–1 when the type was fairly established 181 and to the maturity of the Martin House at Buffalo of 1906 and the Coonley and the Robie Houses of 1907–9.

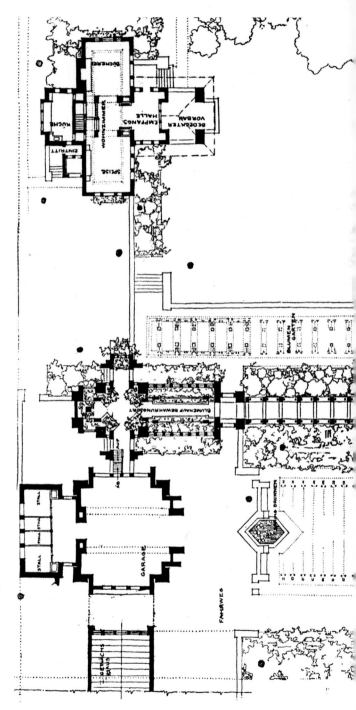

182 Plan of the Martin House, Buffalo, by Frank Lloyd Wright (1903–5). The rooms interlock in a spreading pattern among plantings. There are scarcely any internal doors; instead Wright uses changes of level, columns, and open arches. The servants' quarters, top left, are equally open. The view in ill. 181 is from the far right of this plan

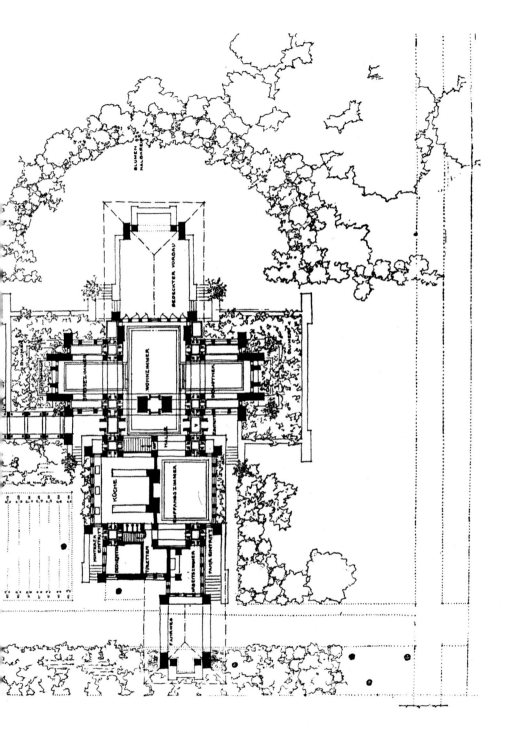

183-4 LEFT AND BELOW Armchairs by Gerrit Rietveld: (left) a restrained cubic shape of pine and leather, designed in 1908 when he was only twenty; (below) an allwood design of 1918–23 – the first piece of furniture embodying the principles of *De Stijl* – where comfort has yielded to geometry

185 Design for terraced housing on the esplanade at Scheveningen, by J. J. P. Oud, 1917

As has already been said, 1910 saw the first publication of Wright's work in Europe, 1914 Gropius's Wright-inspired office range of the exhibition factory at Cologne, 1915 Rob van't Hoff building a complete Wright house in Holland. But Holland very soon abandoned Wright's message and developed Wright's forms in a new spirit. It was the spirit of Cubism. His forms were sufficiently cubic to allow for such a change of meaning. *De Stijl*, the carrier of this transformation, was started in 1917, and its achievements and repercussions are outside the bounds of this book. Its most significant architectural expression at the beginning is Oud's design for seaside housing at Scheveningen, still as simple in the block shapes of the elements as Garnier's in his industrial city. Then almost immediately unfunctional complications were introduced to indicate aesthetically the interaction of planes. Interaction of planes is also the basic aesthetic conception behind Rietveld's famous chair of 1917. It is more ingenious and was more stimulating than his own earlier work, but a chair he did nine years earlier, when he was only twenty, has a *Sachlichkeit* which acquaintance with Cubism could only disturb.

185

184

183

Germany in the first years of the Werkbund was indeed not alone in seeking simplicity and functional form for objects of everyday use. The Dutch contribution began in the first decade of the twentieth century. The Danish contribution began too, and Denmark was to gather strength until some forty years later it had become one of the most important countries in the world in the field of the crafts and industrial design. The furniture and metalwork of Johan Rohde, a painter at first, acquainted with and appreciative of Gauguin, Van Gogh, Toulouse-Lautrec, the Nabis, Toorop, is of great beauty as well as functional soundness. Rohde was led in the direction of design by the Pont-Aven attitude, but realized early that the introduction of figures heavy with symbolic significance was not an answer to the problem of design. His answer is nearer Voysey's, and the cupboard illustrated is as independent of past styles as Voysey at his rare best. Rohde's metalwork was largely

designed for Georg Jensen, the silversmith, and his workshop, and Jensen's own cutlery of the same years shows the identity of approach of the two men.

Of the major nations of Europe only Italy has so far not been mentioned in these pages. Her role during the years here under consideration and up to 1909 had indeed been secondary, in architecture as well as painting and sculpture. Medardo Rosso, it may be argued, mattered internationally, and Sommaruga, D'Aronco, Cattaneo made their *Floreale* in their own way out of elements of the Vienna Secession and the naturalism of French Art Nouveau. But their message was not essentially different from the message of those who had inspired them. The years 1909–14 changed all that. Futurism is one of the constituent movements of the revolution which established the twentieth century, in aesthetic thought, in painting and in architecture. Without Marinetti, Boccioni, Sant'Elia the early twentieth century cannot be described. In architecture, alas, the outbreak of the war and the premature death of Sant'Elia in 1916, prevented anything being actually

built. As in the case of Garnier's *Cité Industrielle* we must go to drawings, to visions of the future. And Sant'Elia's is indeed like Garnier's, a contribution to town planning at least as much as to architecture. In architecture he was the descendant of Vienna and the *Floreale*, though other drawings prove that he was aware of the new rectangularity as well, and of specific Parisian work. Henri Sauvage in 1912–13 in a block of flats, 26 rue Vavin, had conceived the idea of increasing the light in

city streets by stepped-back upper stories. Sant'Elia took up the idea (or recreated it?), and later it became part of the zoning law of New York and an internationally accepted principle. It is an urban, indeed metropolitan, principle, and in this lies its importance, as the importance of Futurism to architecture lies in its adherents' passionate commitment to the city.

186-7 OPPOSITE Danish silverware: teapot and sugar bowl designed by Johan Rohde and made by Georg Jensen (about 1906), and cutlery designed and made in 1908 by Georg Jensen

188 ABOVE Sant'Elia died too young to have any chance of realizing such brilliant Futurist ideas as this, with multi-level traffic (cars below, pedestrian ways linking terraced buildings above), developed sketchily in 1913–14
189 OPPOSITE Sant'Elia's projected skyscraper with recessed storeys, about 1913. There is no ornament

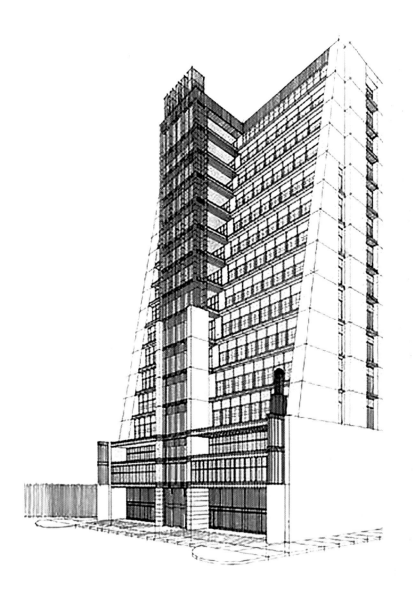

The city was the most urgent and the most comprehensive problem of the nineteenth century. It had been criminally neglected by the architects, and by governments as well. To cut boulevards through Paris had its traffic advantages and offered plenty of spectacular *points de vue* for the placing of monumental buildings, to open up the glacis of the fortress walls of Vienna, to create a generous ring of gardens and ideal sites for yet larger public buildings was no solution. These urban displays had their aesthetic points – and who does not get a visual thrill out of looking up the Avenue de l'Opéra or the Rue Royale? – but the real problem was the visually unpromising one of housing a population which in London (the area which in 1888 became the County of London), grew between 1801 and 1901 from under a million to nearly four and a half million, and in Manchester from about one hundred thousand to about five hundred and fifty thousand. Equally unpromising visually and equally urgent was the problem of the siting of industry. If architects did not care, manufacturers cared only rarely. But Robert Owen, the socialist manufacturer, designed in 1817 a model village with factory and housing, as Ledoux had done twenty years before, and about 1850 the first manufacturers built more modest versions of such schemes, the largest and most convincing being Sir Titus Salt's Saltaire near Leeds which dates from 1850 to about 1870. The huge mill dominates the streets of the workers' houses which are laid

191   out unimaginatively, if acceptably from the purely hygienic point of view. Then came Morris and Norman Shaw, Morris with his fervent sermons of happy labour and social duties, Norman Shaw with his pretty houses of moderate size. And so Bedford Park (see p. 34) was built just outside London in 1875 as the first garden suburb. It was for a middle-class with aesthetic leanings, not for the working-class, but its message could be adapted easily. Make your houses friendly, vary their appearance, leave trees on the site. They were all lessons learned at once, and already in 1888 Port Sunlight was begun outside Liverpool for the employees of Lever's, and in 1895,

192   Bournville for the employees of Cadbury's. In these cases, as at Saltaire, the factory was part of the general scheme. This principle was extended and systematized in Ebenezer Howard's *Tomorrow* which came out in 1898, and again as *Garden Cities of Tomorrow* in 1899. Now the phrase was coined. Let us leave the old cities, vast, dirty, crammed, noisy, and build new ones, to a

190 OPPOSITE Henri Sauvage's flats at 26 rue Vavin, Paris (1912–13); recessed upper storeys and white tile facing give more light to the street

manageable size and a human scale, with their own factories and offices, gardens and spacious parks.

But Howard's was a diagram, the first real garden city, Parker and Unwin's Letchworth, about thirty-five miles north of London, was started in 1904, but yet in 1931 had no more than fifteen thousand inhabitants; and the Hampstead Garden Suburb, started in 1907 and also by Parker and Unwin, was a garden suburb, not a garden city, as was a design by Riemerschmid of 1907 and the Krupps' Margarethenhöhe outside Essen of 1912. The message was unmistakable. The garden city, or what we now call the satellite town,

193

195

191 Saltaire near Leeds, planned in 1850, was the first large industrial housing estate in the world: 820 houses were built in a grid dominated by the mill, the school and the institute, left, and the church, above the mill. The sanitary improvement was great, with service lanes between the rows of houses and a park across the river, but visually Saltaire contributed nothing. (The garden-city housing, top left, is later)

192 Port Sunlight was begun by the firm of Lever's in 1888 on the more human and airy garden suburb pattern: semi-detached houses of brick are scattered among trees so that the town itself is in a park

Towards the International Style

the *Trabantenstadt*, is possible, it is a help even, but it is not the final solution. The big city has come to stay, and we must come to terms with it. That is what Tony Garnier was the first to see. The *Cité Industrielle* is a milestone as much as Howard's *Garden Cities* because, as has already been observed, it is the fiction of a real town on a real site, and because its designer is clearly as interested in its industrial and commercial districts as in its public buildings and houses. Howard's was a social reformer's contribution; Garnier's the potential architect-planner's employed by a government department or a city council; the Futurists' contribution was delirious enthusiasm for exactly that which Howard was running away from.

Here is Marinetti and the Futurist Manifesto of 1909: 'We declare that the splendour of the world has been enriched by a new beauty – the beauty of speed... A roaring, racing car, rattling past like a machine gun, is more beautiful than the Winged Victory of Samothrace... We will sing of the stirring of great crowds – workers, pleasure-seekers, rioters... We will sing the midnight fervour of shipyards blazing with electric moons...' and so on to stations and the smoke of trains, to factories, to bridges, to steamers and finally to aeroplanes. And here is Sant'Elia's *Messaggio* published in the catalogue of his exhibition *Città Nuova* and remodelled by Marinetti to be the Manifesto of Futurist Architecture: 'We must invent and build *ex novo* our modern city like an immense and

193 ABOVE At Letchworth Garden
City, begun in 1904, Parker and
Unwin attempted to do on a large
scale what Shaw's Bedford Park
had done for an élite: the houses
are picturesque variants on the
English cottage style popularized
by Voysey and Baillie Scott,
mixing, brick, tile and roughcast,
in all sizes from single dwellings
to small rows
194 RIGHT Ebenezer Howard,
Design for the Garden City, plan
for the Grand Avenue, 1898

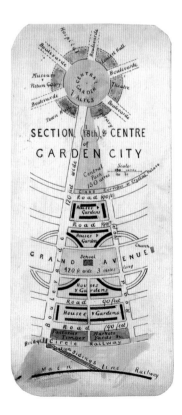

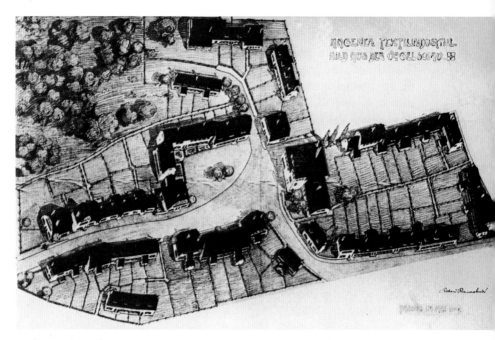

195 TOP The garden suburb became popular throughout Europe, and was the pattern chosen by Richard Riemerschmid; his design for houses for textile workers at Hagen, Westphalia, of 1907, in entire accord with the principles preached by Raymond Unwin

196 ABOVE Tony Garnier, La terrasse sur la vallée, Une cité industrielle, 1917

tumultuous shipyard, active, mobile and everywhere dynamic, and the modern building like a gigantic machine... Lifts must swarm up the façades like serpents of glass and iron. The house of concrete, iron and glass, without ornament ... brutish in its mechanical simplicity ... must rise from the brink of a tumultous abyss, the street ... gathering up the traffic of the metropolis connected for necessary transfers to metal cat-walks and high-speed conveyor belts.'

Perhaps, in spite of Behrens and Gropius, the new style needed someone to grow lyrical over it to win the day. The Futurists provided that. The Expressionists took it on after the war and dreamed up their first steel and all-glass skyscrapers, and finally, only in the middle of the century, the synthesis of the garden city and the metropolitan city was achieved, with garden cities culminating in urban centres, garden estates for ten thousand, with skyscrapers carefully placed, and office buildings in various groupings enclosing patio gardens.

With this, architecture has made a contribution to human life as great as architecture ever did. Is the contribution of painting and sculpture on the same level, and are the so-called fine arts of painting and sculpture and the so-called applied arts of architecture and design working towards the same aims, meeting with the same kind and intensity of response? So it had been in the Middle Ages, so in the Baroque. But that mutual sympathy, that common understanding had not always been a matter of course. The Town Hall of Amsterdam and the *Conspiracy of Claudius Civilis* which Rembrandt painted for it, do not belong together. Those who praised the one would not necessarily praise the other, and if some did they would do it for opposite reasons. Holland in the seventeenth century was a middle-class republic. It was here that the figure of the misunderstood, the neglected, the starving artist first appeared. Moreover, Holland was a Protestant country and not in need of the visual arts for worship. The second age of the art that mattered being unwelcome was the first middle-class age, the nineteenth century, or rather the nineteenth and the later eighteenth century which belongs to it. Neglect grew into active opposition; art on the other hand in Goya, in Blake, in Runge went into a secret language. If you want to understand the artist, you must entrust yourself to him and work at it; he is no longer going to work for you. Patronage in the old sense was dead; what patronage there was to be was as individual, as exposed as the artist's gospel itself. Isolation, half imposed and half self-imposed, was the fate of the painters of Barbizon, of Courbet, of the Impressionists, of the Post-Impressionists. If anything, the pitch of hostility rose. The social development of architecture was bound to be different. There never can be an architect as isolated as a painter. But while this relative security was a gratifying fact for the architect, it was not beneficial for architecture. It meant quite simply that in the nineteenth century the most ruthlessly creative minds did not choose the profession of the architect. This explains to a certain extent the phenomenon of the collapse of aesthetic values in so much of the century. It also explains why it is that the most forward-pointing work so often came from outsiders. The reason why it came from engineers is that the century was one of materialism and hence of science and technology. No century ever before had seen comparable progress in these fields. The progress was made at the expense of aesthetic sensibility of the subtle kind that would have granted acceptance to Impressionism and Post-Impressionism. The Crystal Palace met with success, but so also did the horrors of decorative art displayed in it. Architects' architecture and salon or academy art went together, engineers' and explorers' architecture and explorers' art did not.

But this statement is perhaps too abrupt. The roads followed by the best painters, the best craftsmen or manufacturers and the best architects did occasionally meet. The earliest was the most fruitful meeting; it is that between Morris's preaching and the conversion to craft and design of young painters and young architects. Otherwise meetings were mostly much less significant. One might perhaps just say that the turn to intimacy, the turn away from bombast was of a similar nature in the English Domestic Revival and in Impressionism in painting of the same years. One can perhaps also say that the elegance of façade detail which replaced the grossness and bluster of the High Victorian architects corresponds to the elegance of Impressionist painting as against Courbet's. But that does not take us very far.

It is different with Art Nouveau. Here indeed certain painters were in full accord with the craftsmen-designers. If Art Nouveau is characterized by radical innovation, and by the incantation of the curve, then Gauguin certainly belongs to it – as one of the illustrations to this survey has already demonstrated – and so do the northerners Munch and Toorop and Hodler, and to a more limited degree Maurice Denis, Vallotton, the Seurat of *The Circus*, the Signac of the Fénéon portrait. But after that moment, the short years about 1900, what happened? Architecture went the way of Garnier and Perret, of Loos and Hoffmann, of Behrens and Berg, and design the way of the Werkbund, but painting went the way to Fauvism and Cubism, to the Brücke and the Blaue Reiter, to Futurism and Kandinsky. It is easy to see the similarities of approach and result in Bindesbøll's plates, Gaudí's pinnacles of the Sagrada Familia and Picasso's pottery, but the dates will not match. It is also easy to see as one, cubist paintings of the geometrical kind and cubic architecture of the 1920s – after all Le Corbusier produced both – or Léger's machine men and the machine-worshipers among the architects. But these comparisons are superficial. They do not concern the essential change, which is that architects and designers once more accepted social responsibilities, that architecture and design consequently became a service, and buildings and objects of daily use were designed not only to satisfy the aesthetic wishes of their designers but also to fulfil their practical purposes fully and enthusiastically. Painters and sculptors moved in exactly the opposite direction. They had been cut off from their public already in the nineteenth century. Now they were cut off beyond redemption. Courbet shocked his public because of his message, but that message was perfectly plain to everybody. The Impressionists were attacked for their paintings not being recognizable. But that proved a matter of visual habits. Their aesthetic aims were still those of Titian and Velazquez. Only they had no other than aesthetic aims and that deprived them of the sympathy which the public could extend as long as the spiritual content of a work of art concerned it. To recover these lost spiritual contacts was the most important effort of Gauguin, Van Gogh, the Symbolists, Munch, Hodler – all of them. But they failed, and while from Van Gogh's longing for his paintings to be accepted by simple people, like the broadsheets they read, there might have been a bridge to the architects' and designers' endeavours towards a style for all, there was none from cubism and the dynamic abstract art of Kandinsky.

Gropius hoped there might be, and the Bauhaus made the noble effort of inviting Klee and other abstractionists under its roof. No successful effort has been made since. To offer an abstract artist a wall in a building, or an abstract sculptor a place in a courtyard is no substitute. To force the artist into direct social service against his better aesthetic conviction, as is the principle of Socialist Realism and was that of National-Socialist Realism, is even less of a help. In fact there is no help. The gulf between Jackson Pollock and Mies van der Rohe or even Nervi is beyond bridging. This book is not the place to suggest remedies or foretell the future. Here it must be enough to state that what is most disastrous in the visual arts of the twentieth century and what is most hopeful was fully in existence by the time the Age of the World Wars dawned.

Notes on the Text

1 *The True Principles of Pointed or Christian Architecture*, 1841, p. 1.
2 *Les Beaux-Arts réduits à un même principe*, 1747, p. 47.
3 *The Analysis of Beauty*, Oxford 1955, pp. 32–3.
4 A. Memmi *Elementi dell' Architettura Lodoliana*, Rome 1786, Vol. 1, p. 62.
5 *True Principles*, p. 26.
6–7 *J. of Des. and Manuf.*, IV, 1850, p. 175; I, 1849, p. 80.
8 Redgrave, *Supplementary Report on Design by the Juries ...*, 1852, p. 720.
9 Owen Jones, *The True and the False in the Decorative Arts*, 1863 (lectures given in 1852), p. 14.
10 *J. of Des. and Manuf.*, V, p. 158 and *Supplementary Report on Design*, p. 708.
11 *J. of Des. and Manuf.*, IV, pp. 10, etc., and 74, etc.
12 So Mrs Stanton tells me, quoting from one of the many unpublished letters which will go into her monograph on Pugin.
13 Library Edition, xxxv, p. 47.
14–15 *J. of Des. and Manuf.*, IV, as before; VI, p. 16.
16–23 *Entretiens*: I, 451; I, 472; II, 289; I, 388; I, 321; II, 114; II, 67; II, 55.
24 *Remarks on Secular and Domestic Architecture, Present and Future*, 1858, pp. 224 and 109.
25 *The Seven Lamps of Architecture* The Lamp of Obedience, par. IV and V.
26 *Collected Works*, xxii, 315; 27 *Collected Works*, xxii, 15; 28 *Collected Works*, xxii, 11.
29 J. W. Mackail, *The Life of William Morris*, World's Classics, II, 15.
30–43 *Collected Works*, xxii, 9; xxii, 25; xx, 40 and 42; xxii, 40; xxii, 33; xxii, 42; xxii, 46; xxii, 26; xxiii, 145–6; xxii, 22; xxii, 23–4; xxii, 47; xxii, 335; xxii, 48.
44–45 J. W. Mackail, loc. cit., I, 116; II, 24.
46–47 *Collected Works*, xxii, 73; xxii, 41.
48 *Kindergarten Chats*, edn. of 1947, 187.

49 Quoted from a remarkably early source, the *Drawing Book of the School of Design*, by the Romantic or Nazarene painter William Dyce, published in 1842–3. The passage in question was reprinted in the *Journal of Des. and Manuf.*, VI, 1852.
50 Both quotations in S. Tschudi Madsen: *Sources of Art Nouveau*, Oslo/New York, 1956, pp. 177 and 178.
51 *Les Formules de la Beauté architectonique moderne*, Brussels, 1923, pp. 65–6.
52 *The Studio*, I, 1893, 236.
53 The only evidence is a caption in *The Studio* of 1899, and there are intrinsic reasons against too early a date.
54 Quoted from Madsen, loc. cit., 300. The pieces are now in the V&A (formerly the Bethnal Green Museum) and are as follows: by Gallé a tray, a work-table, a screen and a commode, by Majorelle three cabinets, a tea-table, an armchair and two trays, by Gaillard a chair, by Christiansen a stool, by A. Darras three chairs, by Pérol Frères a wardrobe, a bedstead and a commode, by E. Baguès a writing-table, an armchair, a chair and a stool, by Jallot a chair, and in addition panelling and settle by the Germans J. J. Graf and Spindler and a chair designed by Eckmann for Bing.
55 *Zweckmassig oder phantasievoll.*, quoted from H. Seling and others: *Jugendstil*, Heidelberg and Munich, 1959, pp. 417–18.
56 *Ins Leere gesprochen*, 1897–1900, Innsbruck, 1932, p. 18.
57 *Stilarchitektur...*, pp. 42–3; *Jahrbuch Deutschen Werkbundes*, 1913, p. 30.
58 M. Christophe Pawlowski in his book on Tony Garnier (Centre de Recherche d'Urbanisme, Paris 1967) proves that some of the architecturally most striking buildings of the *Cité Industrielle* do not belong to the work done by Garnier in Rome in 1901–4 but were added before the publication of the scheme in form of a book in 1917. This applies e.g. to the station, the assembly halls and the theatre. On the other hand, the station in the ground-plan of 1901–4 has already the long fingers, and these can only be interpreted as covered arrival and departure bays for cars, cabs, lorries, etc. This being so, they had very probably already the thin far-projecting concrete roofs on slim supports.
59 See C. S. Whitney in *Journal of the Concrete Institute*, Vol. 49, 1953, p. 524.
60 *Erinnerungen an Sturm und Bauhaus*, Munich 1956, p. 154.
61 *Moderne Architektur*, Vienna 1896, p. 41.
62 *Reports from Committees*, 1836, IX, pp. 29, etc.
63 *Supplementary Report on Design*, p. 708.
64 *Essays and Lectures*, 4th ed., 1913, p. 178. The lecture was given in 1882.

Biographical Notes

Berg, Max (1870–1947). As architect to the town of Breslau he designed the Centenary Hall for the 1913 exhibition. Later he withdrew from architecture. *See ills 157, 158.*

Berlage, Hendricus Petrus (1856–1934). Dutch architect, studied with Semper and then in Italy. He placed great importance on the honest use of materials, especially brick. His influence was strongest in the Netherlands, where he published and lectured, and was charged with planning the enlargement of The Hague (1907–8) and Amsterdam (from 1913). *See ill. 117.*

Bernard, Emile (1868–1941). French painter and craftsman. In 1888 during a stay at Pont-Aven with Gauguin he abandoned academic art and Impressionism to turn to Synthetism or Cloisonnism. From 1905 to 1910 he defended his theories in *La Rénovation esthétique*. Much of his work at Pont-Aven belongs to proto-Art Nouveau. Later his art became more conventional. *See ill. 46.*

Bindesbøll, Thorvald (1846–1908). Danish designer. An architect by training, Bindesbøll designed furniture, silver, leatherwork, etc. However, he is most important as a ceramic artist. Under the influence of Far Eastern art he developed a very individual style which is abstract and independent and of a timeless spontaneity. *See ills 48, 49.*

Boussiron, Simon (1873–1958). French engineer. He began in the office of Eiffel, but left it in 1899 and spent the rest of his life exploiting the use of reinforced concrete. *See ill. 155.*

Bunning, James B. (1802–63). In 1843 he was appointed Clerk of the City's Works for London. He built the Coal Exchange, and also Holloway Prison, 1852, and the Metropolitan Cattle Market (Caledonian Market), 1855. *See ill. 5.*

Charpentier, Alexandre (1856–1909). French sculptor and designer. Charpentier was a member of the *Cinq*, and then of the *Six* group. He was famous for his furniture and the bronze plaques which he often used for furniture and bookbindings. *See ill. 76.*

Contamin, V. (1840–93). French engineer. Contamin collaborated with Dutert in the building of the famous *Hall des Machines* at the Paris Exhibition of 1889, which set the stamp on the triumph of iron and steel in modern construction and spread the knowledge of its multifarious possibilities. *See ill. 8.*

Cranach, Wilhelm Lucas von (born 1861). German painter of portraits and landscapes; he also made models of castles. Under the influence of the Russian Julovsky he created *objets d'art. See ill. 66.*

Ashbee, Charles Robert (1863–1942). English architect, designer and author, Ashbee was a pupil of Bodley. He founded the Guild and School of Handicraft in 1888. He exhibited regularly at the Arts and Crafts exhibitions and also at the Vienna Secession. The Guild was discontinued owing to the First World War. *See ill. 124.*

Baker, Sir Benjamin (1840–1907). English engineer. In 1891 he began his long association with John Fowler. They were jointly responsible for the London Metropolitan Railway, and various stations and bridges. Their greatest work was the Forth Bridge; both were knighted at its opening in 1890. Baker was also consulted for the Aswan Dam and designed the vessel in which Cleopatra's needle was brought to London. *See ill. 144.*

Baudot, Anatolede (1834–1915). French architect and theoretician. De Baudot was a pupil of Labrouste and Viollet-le-Duc. As an Inspector of Historic Monuments he carried out the restoration of numerous ancient buildings, and as a government architect he was responsible for a great deal of varied building. As a teacher he defined the use of reinforced materials along the lines he had himself employed at St-Jean de Montmartre. *See ills 145, 146.*

Behrens, Peter (1868–1940). German architect, decorator, painter, modeller, engraver and designer of type. He started within the *Jugendstil*, but by 1904 had emancipated himself from it and turned towards a rational cubic style. In 1907 he was made consultant to the AEG for which he designed his best buildings. He became director of the Düsseldorf School of Applied Arts in 1903 and Professor of Architecture at the Vienna Academy in 1922. *See ills 170, 174–6.*

203

Daum, the brothers Auguste (1853–1909) and Antonin (1864–1930). French glass-workers. Stimulated by the success of Gallé at the Paris Exhibition of 1889, they began to produce glassware in their works at Nancy, and after the Chicago Exhibition in 1893 their work achieved an international reputation. *See ills 71, 74.*

Dutert, Ferdinand (1854–1906). French architect. A pupil of Lebas and Ginain, Dutert concerned himself with the rational use of iron in building. *See ill. 8.*

Eckmann, Otto (1865–1902). German typographer and designer. In 1894 he adopted the *Jugendstil* in his typographical creations. His version of Art Nouveau is one in which vegetable forms are prominent. In 1895-7 he contributed to *Pan.* In his furniture structure is given its due emphasis. *See ills 59, 60, 80.*

Eiffel, Gustave (1832–1923). French engineer. Eiffel is above all famous for his use of iron and steel. Thanks to a combination of precise calculations and a keen feeling for function, Eiffel's work is in the main line of rationalist architectural development in France. *See ills 142, 143.*

Endell, August (1871–1925). German designer. He studied philosophy and as an artist he was self-taught. He was at first inspired by Obrist. In 1896 he built the Atelier Elvira, in Munich. Later he was Director of the Breslau Academy. *See ills 87, 89.*

Fowler, Sir John (1817–1898). English engineer, best known for his work on railways. Set up his own business in 1844, and became engineer to the London Metropolitan Railway. In 1865 he became president of the Institute of Civil Engineers – its youngest ever. He worked with Baker *(q.v.)* on the Forth Bridge, completed in 1887. From 1871 he was general engineering adviser to the Khedive Ismail of Egypt. *See ill. 144.*

Gaillard, Eugène (1862–1933). French furniture designer, one of the collaborators of Samuel Siegfried Bing. *See ill. 78.*

Gallé, Emile (1846–1904). French craftsman and designer. After brilliantly pursuing classical studies he worked in the pottery and glass works of his father. He took part in the Exhibition of 1878, at which his technical mastery and originality became known. He is one of the chief exponents of Art Nouveau, his specialities being glass and furniture. *See ills 37, 39, 75.*

Garnier, Tony (1869–1948). French architect, engineer and theorist. Garnier won the Prix de Rome in 1899. While in Italy he designed his *Cité Industrielle.* In 1904 Edouard Hériot, the new mayor of Lyons, Garnier's native city, discovered him and entrusted to him the municipal works department. *See ills 151-4.*

Gaudí Y Cornet, Antoni (1852–1926). The greatest of Art Nouveau architects. Most of his buildings are in Barcelona and are mentioned in the test. His chief early works are the Casa Vicens of 1878, and the Palau Güell of 1884-9. The mature works are Sta Coloma de Cervelló (begun 1898), the Güell Park (begun 1900), the upper parts of the transept façade of the Sagrada Familia (begun 1903) and the Casa Batlló and Casa Milá (begun 1905). He lived a modest, retired life, wholly dedicated to his work. *See ills 52, 83–6, 102–109.*

Gauguin, Paul (1848–1903). At first in banking, he gave up his job to devote himself wholly to painting. He contributed to the last Impressionist shows. In 1886 he made his first stay at Pont-Aven. Anxious to get away from modern civilization he left for Martinique in 1887. During a second stay at Pont-Aven with Emile Bernard and others he developed a style of tapestry-like two-dimensionality with simple and unbroken colours which sometimes comes near to Art Nouveau, sometimes to the Expressionism of the 1920s. He also did sculpture of a deliberately primitive kind. In 1888 he stayed for some months at Arles with Van Gogh. He then returned to Pont-Aven, but in 1891 left for good to live on Tahiti. A last visit to France (August 1893–February 1895) preceded his final stay in Tahiti which he left only for the even greater solitude of the Marquesas Islands where he died. *See ills 40–45.*

Gilbert, Alfred (1854–1934). Sculptor. Among his best-known works are the Clarence Memorial at Windsor (begun in 1892) and the Shaftesbury Memorial Fountain *(Eros)*, Piccadilly. Already in the 1880s his style is near Art Nouveau, but of a wholly personal variety. *See ills 50, 51.*

Gimson, Ernest (1864–1920). English craftsman and designer, studied architecture from 1881 to 1884. On the advice of William Morris he joined J. D. Sedding, remaining with him from 1886 to 1888. From 1901 on he designed furniture and metalwork. His designs were executed by a group of craftsmen at Cirencester, and subsequently in his own workshops – the Daneway House Workshops. *See ill. 122.*

Gropius, Walter (Born 1883). Studied architecture in Munich and Berlin 1903-7. In 1919 succeeded Van de Velde in Weimar at the art school, which he converted into the famous Bauhaus. The Bauhaus, with a teaching staff composed of men like Klee, Kandinsky, Feininger, Schlemmer and

Moholy-Nagy, rapidly became one of the great centres of the International Modern movement. It removed to Dessau in 1925. Gropius left it in 1928 and was replaced by Mies van der Rohe. In 1933 the school was disbanded, and its members dispersed in the face of the Nazi storm. Gropius went as a refugee first to England, then to the USA, where he taught at Harvard. Gropius is one of the creators of the style of the twentieth century, which appears already complete in his Fagus factory of 1911. He is also the most impressive speaker of the social duties and responsibilities of the architect. *See ill. 176.*

Guimard, Hector (1867–1942). French architect and decorator. Guimard adopted the ideas of Art Nouveau, of which he was one of the chief representatives in France. He was responsible for the famous entrances to the Métro in Paris, and also designed a number of houses in the west end of Paris, chief among them the Castel Béranger of 1897–8. *See ills 96–101.*

Hennebique, François (1842–1921). French engineer. Was a contractor at Courtrai and Brussels before he went to Paris. From 1879–88 he worked on the combination of iron and concrete, and in 1892 he took out patents. He became the leading French designer and contractor for reinforced concrete. His factories of the nineties are of straightforward post and lintel construction, but the house he designed for himself in 1904 is a folly built to display the virtues of concrete. *See ill. 147.*

Hoentschel, Georges (1855–1915). French designer and decorator. Hoentschel was given the job of designing the pavilion of the Union Centrale des Arts Décoratifs at the Exhibition of 1900. *See ill. 68.*

Hoffmann, Josef (1870–1956). Austrian architect and interior designer. A pupil of Otto Wagner, Hoffmann was one of the founders of the Vienna Secession. In 1903 he co-founded the *Wiener Werkstätte*, and for the next thirty years it was inspired by him. He began in the Art Nouveau, but by about 1900–1 he had turned away from it to a style of squares and rectangles, largely inspired by Mackintosh. His Convalescent Home at Purkersdorf of 1903 shows this style fully developed, and his Palais Stoclet in Brussels of 1905 demonstrated for the first time that within the style of the twentieth century, monumentality and exquisite elegance could be achieved. *See ills 140, 163, 164.*

Holabird, William (1854–1923). American architect of the Chicago School, trained by W. Le Baron Jenney and then in the office of Burnham & Root. In partnership with Martin Roche he pioneered the structural and expressive use of the steel frame in office buildings, devising large broad windows with fixed centre and movable sides for better ventilation ('Chicago windows'). *See ill. 25.*

Horta, Victor (1861–1947). Belgian architect. Horta built his first houses in 1886. Three years later he began to use iron in architectural construction, which permitted him to introduce curves into both his interiors and exteriors. His key works are the Hôtel Tassel of 1892, the Hôtel Solvay of 1895, etc., and the Maison du Peuple of 1896–9, all in Brussels. Later he abandoned the Art Nouveau originality displayed by these buildings and went over to classicism. *See ills 88, 90–4.*

Jensen, Georg (1866–1935). Danish goldsmith, Jensen was also a sculptor and a ceramic artist. After a stay in Paris (1900–1) he started to make jewelry in collaboration with Magnus Ballin. About 1904 he began to concentrate on silverware. His fame spread almost at once, and had become international by 1910. *See ills 190, 191.*

Klimt, Gustav (1862–1918). Austrian painter. After conventional beginnings he suddenly, in 1899, appeared with an Art Nouveau style distinctly his own. He took an active part in the Vienna Secession, and became its President. The relationship between decoration and architecture remained one of his major preoccupations and his influence on the decorative arts in Austria was considerable. In painting, both Kokoschka and Schiele were inspired by him. His *magnum opus* in decoration is the mosaics in Hoffmann's Palais Stoclet. *See ill. 166.*

Koepping, Karl (1848–1914). German painter and glass designer. After studying chemistry he turned to painting in 1869. From 1896 on he contributed to *Pan*. He made a collection of Japanese *objets d'art* and took inspiration from his collection for his glass vases, etc., which are his chief title to fame. *See ill. 72.*

Labrouste, Henri (1801–75). French architect. He was awarded the Prix de Rome at the age of twenty-three, and spent five years in Italy. He became the leader of the Rationalist school as opposed to the Academy. His use of iron exposed inside the Bibliothèque Ste-Geneviéve in Paris in 1843–50 heralded a revolution in architecture. *See ill. 6.*

Lalique, René (1860–1945). French jeweller and glass-worker. Lalique studied at the Beaux-Arts in Paris where he founded his glass workshops. His forms and designs were based on floral motifs. He collaborated with Samuel Siegfried Bing. *See ills 64, 65, 67.*

Lemmen, Georges (1865–1916). Belgian painter and graphic designer, son of an architect. In 1899 he joined *Les Vingt*, then the *Libre Esthétique*, and designed posters as well as exhibiting his own work. He collaborated with Van de Velde and Van Rysselberghe in the revival of decorative arts in Belgium. *See ill. 58.*

Lethaby, William Richard (1857–1931). English architect. Wrote books of great importance on the theory and history of architecture. He was responsible with Sir George Frampton for the establishment of the Central School of Arts and Crafts, whose principal he was from 1893 to 1911. He designed the Eagle Insurance Building in Birmingham in 1900, and the church at Brockhampton in 1900–2. *See ill. 120.*

Leveillé, Ernest Baptiste. French craftsman in ceramics and glass. He was a pupil of Rousseau. In 1889 he won a Gold Medal at the *Exposition Universelle. See ill. 38.*

Loos, Adolf (1870–1933). Austrian architect. Studied in Dresden and then visited the United States. From 1897 onwards he adopted a style which eschewed all ornament and sought to obtain its effects by the articulation of planes and the use of beautiful materials. Loos was not a successful architect, and his buildings are few. In 1922–7 he lived in Paris and then he returned to Vienna. *See ill. 165.*

Lutyens, Sir Edwin Landseer (1869–1944). English architect. His early architecture was influenced by Shaw, Voysey and the Arts and Crafts but possesses a boldness entirely his own. From 1906 he turned to Palladianism and Neo-Georgianism. Architect of New Delhi, the British Embassy building in Washington and the Cenotaph in Whitehall. *See ill. 117.*

Macdonald, the sisters Margaret (1865–1933) and Frances (1874–1921). English craftswomen. Margaret Macdonald was a designer and worker in metals, stained glass and embroidery. In 1900 she married Charles Rennie Mackintosh and collaborated with him in much of his work. Both sisters trained at the Glasgow School of Art, and Frances was a teacher there from 1907 on wards. She worked sometimes alone and sometimes in collaboration with her sister. In 1899 she married J. H. McNair and collaborated with him in the designing of furniture and stained glass. *See ill. 127.*

Mackintosh, Charles Rennie (1868–1928). Scottish architect and designer. Studied at the Glasgow School of Art. Assistant and later partner in the firm of Honeyman and Keppie. The commission to build the Glasgow School of Art which he was given in 1897 made his fame. His principal works are all between 1897 and about 1905. They are Windyhill, Kilmacolm (1899–1901), Hill House, Helensburgh (1902–4), tea rooms for Miss Cranston (1896–1911) and the Scotland Street School (1904–5). Mackintosh and his group exhibited in Vienna in 1900 and in Turin in 1902. *See ills 125–37, 140, 141.*

Mackmurdo, Arthur Heygate (1851–1942). English architect and designer. Mackmurdo travelled with Ruskin to Italy. In 1882 he founded the Century Guild, and two years later he also founded the journal *Hobby Horse.* From *c.* 1883 he designed furniture, wallpaper, textiles and metalwork. In 1904 he abandoned architecture in order to devote himself completely to social theories. *See ills 28, 29, 33, 34, 110–12.*

Maillart, Robert (1872–1940). Swiss engineer, inventor of the 'mushroom piers' which unite in one member the function of load and support. In 1901 he began to apply his principles to the bridges that made him famous. *See ill. 156.*

Majorelle, Louis (1859–1929). French furniture designer. After studying in Paris, Majorelle took over the ceramics workshop of his father. The success of Gallé led him to abandon period imitation for original work. His most interesting pieces date from around the time of the Exhibition of 1900 in Paris. *See ill. 77.*

Morris, William (1834–96). English designer, craftsman, poet and social reformer, the fountain-head of the rebirth of the crafts and of the sense of the social responsibilities of artist and architect. Morris was initially inspired by Ruskin. He began to take an interest in craft and design when he built a house for himself in 1859. His own firm was founded in 1861, and in 1877 he started on his long series of lectures on art and social problems. His influence was immense. The last of the crafts he tried his hand at was the art of the book (Kelmscott Press, founded 1890). *See ills 9, 11–13, 29, 73.*

Nyrop, Martin (1849–1925). Danish architect. Nyrop used traditional motifs but experimented with the use of cast iron. *See ill. 119.*

Obrist, Hermann (1863–1927). Swiss sculptor and designer. First studied science and then art, including sculpture. In 1892 he started an embroidery workshop in Florence and moved it to Munich in 1894. He was one of the founders of the *Vereinigte Werkstätten für Kunst und Handwerk* in Munich. His works are few but influential. In the field of sculpture the most important piece is the model for an all-but-abstract monument done *c.* 1900. *See ill. 55.*

Olbrich, Joseph Maria (1867–1908). Austrian architect, craftsman and book-designer. Travelled to Rome and Tunisia, then studied with Otto Wagner in Vienna. Co-founder, with Klimt, of the Secession whose building he designed. Called by the Grand Duke of Hesse to Darmstadt, where he designed the Mathildenhöhe artists' colony. *See ill. 138.*

Oud, Jacobus Johannes Pieter (1890–1963). Dutch architect, member of *De Stijl.* He specialized in housing schemes (e.g. as City Architect of Rotterdam, 1918) and pioneered the International Style, admiring Berlage's functionalism and truth to materials. Later he renounced strict functionalism, but remained concerned with human needs in architecture. *See ill. 185.*

Parker, Barry. See Unwin, Sir Raymond.

Paxton, Sir Joseph (1801–65). English horticulturalist. In 1826 he became superintendent of the Duke of Devonshire's gardens at Chatsworth. In 1836 he began to erect a great conservatory 90 metres (300 ft) in length, which was completed in 1840, and enabled Paxton in 1850 to design for the Great Exhibition the Crystal Palace, a building entirely of glass and iron and the first ever erected by the technique of prefabrication. *See ill. 2.*

Perret, the brothers Auguste (1874–1954) and Gustave (1875–1952). French builders, i.e. contractors for architectural work. They were the first to use reinforced concrete in the architecture of private buildings, and they developed its use both structurally and aesthetically. They kept away, however, from any utilization of the possibilities of concrete for wide spans and bold cantilevering. Their vision of architecture was still that of the classical styles of post and lintel. The principal works are the house in the rue Franklin of 1902, the garage in the rue de Ponthieu of 1905, the church of Notre Dame at Raincy of 1922–3 and the new buildings at Le Havre erected from 1945 onwards as part of a plan of reconstruction. *See ills 148–50.*

Prior, Edward Schroder (1852–1932). English architect, the most original in the Arts and Crafts group. Professor at Cambridge from 1912 to 1932. He also produced some outstanding books on English medieval architecture. *See ill. 116.*

Prouvé, Victor (1858–1943). French painter, engraver, sculptor and decorator, Prouvé studied in Nancy and Paris and subsequently worked for Gallé. After Gallé's death he was appointed President of the Nancy School where he continued his work until after the First World War. *See ills 63, 70, 74.*

Richardson, Henry Hobson (1838–86). American architect, studied at the Beaux-Arts in Paris and worked for Labrouste before returning to the United States. He built churches, offices, public buildings and houses in a massive free Romanesque style (the major exception is the shingled Stoughton House at Cambridge, Mass.). Office buildings such as the Marshall Field Wholesale Store in Chicago (1885–7) influenced the Chicago School. *See ill. 22.*

Riemerschmid, Richard (1868–1957). German painter, then architect. In 1897 he was one of the founders of the *Vereinigte Werkstätten für Kunst und Handwerk* and he took part in the Paris Exhibition of 1900. He was Director of the School for Decorative Arts in Munich from 1912 to 1924, and in 1926 became Director of the Cologne *Werkschule.* His most important architectural achievement was the interior of the Munich *Schauspielhaus* (1901); his designs for furniture are among the most progressive of their day. *See ills 81, 167–9, 173, 195.*

Rietveld, Gerrit Thomas (1888–1964). Dutch architect and furniture designer. Trained first as a cabinet-maker, then as an architect, he joined *De Stijl* and throughout his career maintained an interest in interior design. *See ills 183, 184.*

Roche, Martin (1855–1927). American architect, trained in Chicago by W. Le Baron Jenney. As partner of William Holabird *(q.v.)* he specialized in interiors. *See ill. 25.*

Rohde, Johan (1856–1935). Danish designer. At first a painter, and considerably influenced by Maurice Denis, he later turned to designing furniture and silverware. As a collaborator with Jensen *(q.v.),* he had a decisive influence on Danish design. *See ill. 187.*

Rousseau, Eugène (1827–91). French craftsman in ceramics and glass. Rousseau's works are far less known than they deserve to be. What he did in the mid-eighties is among the most daringly novel work anywhere in Europe. *See ills 35, 36.*

Sant'Elia, Antonio (1880–1916). Italian architect and theorist. His early work was influenced by the Vienna School. He was fascinated by the city and exhibited his vision of the future, the *Città Nuova*, at Milan in 1914. A socialist, he never fully shared the aims of Futurism, with which his name is associated. He was killed in the First World War, and only one of his designs was ever built, a house in Como. *See ills 188, 189.*

Sauvage, Henri (1873–1932). French architect. Sauvage collaborated with Frantz Jourdain on the Samaritaine building and was responsible for numerous modern buildings in Paris, including the house at no. 26 rue Vavin of 1912–13. *See ill. 190.*

Sehring, Bernhard (1855–1932). German architect. Sehring is primarily known for the theatres he built, for instance those of Düsseldorf, Bielefeld and Berlin, but his most interesting building is the Tietz Store in the Leipziger Strasse in Berlin of 1898, with its expanses of sheer glass. *See ill. 95.*

Shaw, Richard Norman (1831–1912). Side by side with Webb the chief reformer of domestic architecture in England. His style was inspired by the English seventeenth-century vernacular of the Home Counties, by seventeenth-century Dutch architecture and the William and Mary and Queen Anne styles in England. His influence was wide and wholesome. His style was complete by 1866–7 (Glen Andred, also Bingley church), but the climax was in the mid-seventies with New Zealand Chambers in the City of London, his own house in Hampstead, Swan House in Chelsea and such country houses as Adcote. About 1890 he changed allegiance and went classical and at the same time grander than he had been before (Chesters 1891, Piccadilly Hotel 1905). *See ills 15, 17, 18.*

Sullivan, Louis (1856–1924). American architect. Sullivan studied at the Ecole des Beaux-Arts in Paris under Vaudremer. He was a true precursor of modern architecture, though his stature was recognized only after his death. Frank Lloyd Wright was trained under him from 1887 to 1893. Sullivan's key works are the Auditorium Building in Chicago (1887–9), memorable chiefly for its feathery ornament, and the cellular Wainwright Building at St Louis (1890) and Guaranty Building at Buffalo (1894–5). The acme is the Carson Pirie Scott store in Chicago of 1899–1904. *See ills 24, 26, 27, 179.*

Taut, Bruno (1880–1938). German architect. His exhibition building of 1914 is by far his most daring work. Later, for a short time, he designed in the spirit of the then potent German Expressionism. Soon, however, he fell in with the Berlin group of those believing in the International Modern (housing estates, Berlin, especially the Britz estate). He was made city architect at Magdeburg and there introduced strong colours in the façades of terrace houses. In 1932 he was invited to Moscow, and from there went to Japan, finally was professor at Istanbul. *See ills 177, 179.*

Telford, Thomas (1757–1834). English civil engineer. The son of a shepherd and first apprenticed to a stonemason, he later became Shropshire County Surveyor. He is famous as the builder of canals, aqueducts, roads and bridges both in England and Scotland. In 1820 he was made the first president of the Institute of Civil Engineers. *See ill. 4.*

Tiffany, Louis Comfort (1848–1933). The most famous of American craftsmen, designers and entrepreneurs in the Arts and Crafts. His father owned a store famous for elegance and incorporating a silverware department. The son set up on his own in 1879. He quickly became famous for interior decoration, stained glass (the Tiffany Glass Company was incorporated in 1886), and then his exquisite Art Nouveau Favrile glass, introduced about 1894 and very soon handled by Bing in Paris. While Favrile is wholly original, Tiffany's interiors show the influence of Morris and of the Early Christian and Italian Romanesque styles. *See ill. 71.*

Unwin, Sir Raymond (1863–1940) and Parker, Barry (1867–1947). English architects and town planners. In 1904 they were commissioned to design Letchworth, the first of the garden-cities, and in 1907 the Hampstead Garden Suburb. Raymond Unwin's book *Town Planning in Practice* greatly influenced his own and the next generation. *See ill. 193.*

Vallin, Eugène (1856–1922). French designer of furniture and façades (for the architect Biet). Vallin served his apprenticeship at Nancy. He produced a good deal for Gothic and neo-Gothic churches, decidedly under the influence of Viollet-le-Duc. In 1895 he freed himself from period imitation and turned to the Art Nouveau of Nancy. His furniture keeps a balance between emphasis on abstract curves and motifs from nature. *See ill. 74.*

Van de Velde, Henry (1863–1957). Van de Velde began in Belgium as a painter, but around 1893 he turned to architecture and craftsmanship. In 1896 Bing asked him to furnish a room in his shop 'L'Art Nouveau', and in 1897 he exhibited at Dresden. His success in Germany was such that he settled there in 1899. In 1901 he was called to Weimar as consultant to the Grand Duke. In 1906 he became head of the Weimar School of Applied Arts which later became the Bauhaus. His principal works are the Werkbund Theatre in 1914 in Cologne, and the Kröller-Müller Museum at Otterlo (1937–53). He is equally important as a theoretical writer. He began to put down his theories in 1894 and had by then already demonstrated his abstract, linear, tensile style in book decoration. His furniture has the same qualities. *See ills 44, 54, 59, 79.*

Viollet-le-Duc, Eugène Emmanuel (1814–79). French architect and theorist. He was the leading European restorer of historic buildings, but also designed churches and flats. His writings were less traditionalist and far more influential than his work. *See ill. 53.*

Voysey, Charles F. Annesley (1857–1941). Voysey is the most important English architect and designer of the generation after Morris. He was a pupil of Seddon and then of Devey. In the eighties he designed wallpapers and textiles; from 1889 houses. Within ten years he had established himself as a favourite architect of country houses, all of them comfortable, informal, and only in the most general way still adhering to historicism, i.e. the Tudor vernacular. Voysey's designs, carried out by factories, not by craftsmen, are of great freshness and crispness and had much influence on the Continent. *See ills 56, 57, 113–5, 121, 124.*

Wagner, Otto (1841–1918). Appointed Professor at the Vienna Academy in 1894, Wagner was already well known as an architect inspired by the Italian Renaissance. His book *Moderne Architektur* was based on his inaugural lecture and became a classic of the architectural revolution. His buildings between 1898 and 1904 are in a heavy Art Nouveau, inspired by the Baroque and to a certain extent by his pupil Olbrich (Vienna Metro, Hofpavillon and Karlsplatz stations, and unexecuted designs for public buildings). In 1904 he abandoned lush curves, and in the Vienna Postal Savings Bank of 1905 achieved one of the masterpieces of early twentieth-century rationalism. *See ills 159, 161.*

Webb, Philip (1831–1915). English architect and designer. Red House and Webb's country houses after it, such as Joldwyns of 1873, Smeaton Manor of 1878, Standen of 1892, the larger and more idiosyncratic Rounton Grange of 1872–6, and Clouds of 1881–91, had as much influence as Shaw's houses, both in England and abroad. Webb built one church, Brampton in Cumberland, before 1874. He also designed furniture and metalwork. *See ills 9, 11, 16, 73.*

Whistler, James Abbot McNeill (1834–1903). American painter. He was trained in Paris, and after 1859 lived mainly in London. Whistler was greatly influenced by Japanese art, which he collected, and his interior decoration schemes – probably inspired by his friend Edward Godwin – were revolutionary in their simplicity and use of plain, pale colours. He decorated Oscar Wilde's house in Tite Street and, more elaborately, the 'Peacock Room' of the Leyland house. His own house in Tite Street, by Edward Godwin (1878) was strikingly original with an asymmetrical white-painted exterior and yellow and white rooms. In his paintings, which shocked Ruskin, Whistler combined Impressionism with echoes of Japanese wood-cuts. *See ills 29, 30.*

White, Stanford (1853–1906). American architect. Worked under H. H. Richardson in the designing of Trinity Church in Boston. Joined McKim and Mead and was the most brilliant designer in the partnership. *See ill. 21.*

Wiener, René (1856–1939). A member of a family of Nancy bookbinders and a bookbinder himself. He abandoned period imitation and applied the process of pyrogravure to the working of leather, collaborating for instance with Toulouse-Lautrec and Victor Prouvé. His best years are the nineties. *See ills 62, 63.*

Willumsen, Jens Ferdinand (1863–1958). Danish painter and sculptor. During his stays in Paris (1888–9, 1890–4) Willumsen was powerfully influenced by Gauguin and Bernard in their Pont-Aven style, and he exhibited with the Independents. In 1890 he met Redon, and that also left its mark on Willumsen's work. *See ill. 47.*

Wright, Frank Lloyd (1869–1959). American architect. Wright was in the office of Louis Sullivan from 1887 to 1893 and then, in the first decade of the new century, designed his most important buildings, the Larkin Building at Buffalo (1906), the Unity Church at Oak Park, Chicago (1906), and houses such as the Martin House, Buffalo (1903–5) and the Coonley (1907) and Robie (1909) Houses at Chicago. Two publications of his work in Berlin in 1910 and 1911 inaugurated his influence on Europe. His houses are characterized by low spreading plans, cantilevered roofs and interpenetration of the internal spaces. His largest buildings up to the twenties were the Imperial Hotel at Tokyo (1916–22) and Midway Garden, Chicago (1914). Here a passion for angular, abstract ornament and fanciful detail comes to the fore, and was to dominate much of his later work (Hollyhock House, Los Angeles 1920, Price Tower, Bartlesville 1953–6). He rarely fits into the pattern of the socalled International Modern (Falling Water, 1936). The most prominent buildings of his old age are the two for the Johnson Wax Company at Racine, Wis. (1936–9, 1950) and the Guggenheim Museum in New York (1956–9), a monument to its architect rather than a functional museum. Frank Lloyd Wright's imagination was of truly Welsh fertility, and remains an inspiration to those who are dissatisfied with rationalism. *See ills 180, 181.*

Sources of Illustrations

1 Photo © John Bethell. All rights reserved 2024/ Bridgeman Images
2 Rijksmuseum, Amsterdam. Object no. RP-F-F25213-U. Photo attributed to Claude M. Ferrier and Friedrich von Martens
3 Photo Ursula Clark/Historic England Archive/ Heritage Image Partnership Ltd/Alamy Stock Photo
4 Photo Hulton Archive/Epics/Getty Images
5 Photo Country Life
6 Musée Carnavalet, Histoire de Paris. Inv. no. PH26546. Photo Charles Joseph Antoine Lansiaux
7 Photo Science and Society Picture Library/ SuperStock
8 Library of Congress, Prints and Photographs Division, Washington, D.C. Call no. LOT 13418, no. 327 [P&P]
9 Photo Andreas von Einsiedel/National Trust Photographic Library/Bridgeman Images
10 Arts Council of Great Britain
11 British Museum, London. Reg. no. 1994,0512.1
12 Cooper Hewitt, Smithsonian Design Museum, New York. Museum purchase from General Acquisitions Endowment. 1985-87-1
13 Photo Victoria and Albert Museum, London. Acc. no. CIRC.291-1953
14 Art Institute of Chicago. Purchased with funds provided by Mrs Theodore D. Tieken. Ref. 1972.390
15 Photo Ian Nairn
16 Photo akg-images/Bildarchiv Monheim
17 National Monuments Record, London. Photo Quentin Lloyd
18 Photo Martin Charles/RIBA Collections. Library ref. MC A 020309
19 Photo Arcaid Images/Alamy Stock Photo
20 Art Institute of Chicago. Gift of Robert A. Taub. Ref. no. 2012.248.19. Photo Frederick H. Evans
21 Library of Congress, Prints and Photographs Division, Washington, D.C. Historic American Buildings Survey. Call no. HABS RI,1-BRIST,18–1. Photo Cervin Robinson

22 Historic New England, Boston. Gift of William Sumner Appleton, 15 June 1934. Ref. no. PC001.01. TMP.209
23 National Monuments Record, London. Photo Quentin Lloyd
24 Library of Congress, Prints and Photographs Division, Washington, D.C. Historic American Buildings Survey. Call no. HABS NY,15-BUF,6–3. Photo Jack E. Boucher
25 Photo Hedrich Blessing Collection/Chicago. History Museum/Getty Images
26 Photo Angelo Hornak/Corbis/Getty Images
27 Library of Congress, Prints and Photographs Division, Washington, D.C. Historic American Buildings Survey. Call no. HABS NY,15-BUF,6–13. Photo Jack E. Boucher
28, 29 Private collection
30 Photo Freer Gallery of Art, Smithsonian Institution, Washington D.C. Gift of Charles Lang Freer/Bridgeman Images
31 Getty Research Institute, Los Angeles. Call no. 9923811490001551
32 Private collection
33 Los Angeles County Museum of Art. Gift of Heidi Wettenhall and Said Saffari through the 2014 Decorative Arts and Design Acquisitions Committee (DA²). M.2014.70.2
34 William Morris Gallery, London Borough of Waltham Forest. Mackmurdo bequest, 1942. Catalogue no. F39
35 Photo Les Arts Décoratifs, Paris/Jean Tholance/ akg-images
36 The Walters Art Museum, Baltimore. Acquired by William T. Walters. Acc. no. 47.384
37 The Metropolitan Museum of Art, New York. Purchase, Edward C. Moore Jr. Gift, 1926. Acc. no. 26.228.8
38 Les Arts Décoratifs, Paris. Inv. no. 5690
39 Les Arts Décoratifs, Paris. Inv. no. 3591
40 Museum für Kunst und Gewerbe, Hamburg. Inv. no. 1978.90
41 Private collection
42 Designmuseum Danmark, Copenhagen
43 Art Institute of Chicago. Regenstein Endowment Fund. Ref. no. 2011.227
44 The Morgan Library & Museum, New York
45 Private collection
46 Hessisches Landesmuseum Darmstadt. Inv. no. Kg 65:18. Photo Wolfgang Fuhrmannek
47 Designmuseum Danmark, Copenhagen. Inv. no. 32/1956. Photo Pernille Klemp
48 Designmuseum Danmark, Copenhagen. Inv. no. B3/1942. Photo Pernille Klemp
49 Designmuseum Danmark, Copenhagen. Inv. no. 1176

124 Victoria and Albert Museum, London.
Acc. no. CIRC.478-1954
125 Photo Sepia Times/Universal Images Group
via Getty Images
126 Photo Christie's Images/Bridgeman Images
127 Photo CSG CIC Glasgow Museums. Collection/
Bridgeman Images
128 Photo Arcaid Images/Alamy Stock Photo
129 National Monuments Record, London. Photo
Quentin Lloyd
130, 131, 133 British Council. Photos Wickham
132 Photo Hulton Fine Art Collection/Culture
Club/Getty Images
134 Photo DeAgostini Picture Library/Getty Images
135 Photo Christie's Images, London/Scala, Florence
136 Photo DeAgostini Picture Library/Scala, Florence
137 The Hill House, Helensburgh
138 Photo akg-images/Erich Lessing
139 © Estate of Josef Hoffmann
140 Private collection
141 The Willow Tea Rooms, Glasgow. Photo
Jacqueline Hyde
142 Photo Look and Learn/Bridgeman Images
143 Musée Carnavalet, Histoire de Paris. Inv. no.
PH73416. Photo Hippolyte Blancard
144 Photo Malindine/Popperfoto/Getty Images
145 Photo © Ministère de la Culture –
Médiathèque du patrimoine et de la photographie,
Dist. RMN-Grand Palais/Yvan Segura-Lara.
© RMN-GP gestion droit d'auteur Ivan Segura-Lara
146 Photo Gilles Targat/Photo12/Alamy Stock Photo
148 Photo © Andrea Jemolo/Bridgeman Images
149 Cité de l'architecture et du patrimoine/Centre
d'archives d'architecture contemporaine, Paris.
Fonds Auguste Perret et Perret frères. 535 AP 911/4
150 Photo © Collection Artedia/Bridgeman Images
151 Musée des Beaux-Arts de Lyon. Don de Mme
Madame Tony Garnier, 1952
152 Bibliothèque municipale de Lyon
153 Bibliothèque municipale de Lyon. Photo by
Icas94/De Agostini/Getty Images
154 Bibliothèque municipale de Lyon
155 Photo courtesy Société des entreprises
Boussiron
156 Photo ETH-Bibliothek Zürich, Bildarchiv.
Hs_1085-1905-6-1-160
157 Photo akg-images
158 Photo Francis Rowland Yerbury/RIBA
Collections. Library ref. Qc45
159 Wien Museum. Inv. no. 47337/9
160 Photo Angelo Hornak/Corbis/Getty Images
161 Photo akg-images/Erich Lessing
162 Photo Angelo Hornak/Alamy Stock Photo
163 Photo brandstaetter images/Getty Images
164 Photo Studio Minders

165 Photo Reiffenstein
166 Museum für angewandte Kunst (MAK), Vienna
167 Photo The Museum of Modern Art, New York/
Scala, Florence. Riemerschmid © DACS 2023
168 Private collection
170 Private collection
171 Kunstgewerbemuseum, Staatliche Museen zu
Berlin. Inv. no. SB 172. Photo Stephan Klonk
172 Photo The Museum of Modern Art, New York/
Scala, Florence. Melva Bucksbaum Purchase Fund.
Obj. no. 24.2000
173 Art Institute of Chicago. Purchased with funds
provided by Mr and Mrs Manfred Steinfeld. Ref.
no. 1986.180
174 Photo Kunstbibliothek, Staatlichen Museen zu
Berlin/Dietmar Katz. Inv. no. 14061857
175, 177 Dr Franz Stoedtner-Archiv
176 Photo Dirk Renckhoff/Alamy Stock Photo
178 Baukunstarchiv, Akademie der Künste, Berlin
179 Photo Hedrich-Blessing Collection/Chicago
History Museum/Getty Images
180 Library of Congress, Prints and Photographs
Division, Washington, D.C. Historic American
Buildings Survey. Call no. HABS ILL,16-CHIG,12–2.
Photo Harold Allen
181 Library of Congress, Prints and Photographs
Division, Washington, D.C. Historic American
Buildings Survey. Call no. HABS NY,15-BUF,5--1
182 Library of Congress, Prints and Photographs
Division, Washington, D.C. Historic American
Buildings Survey. Call no. HABS NY,15-BUF,5--9
183 Photo © Centraal Museum Utrecht/Axel
Funke. Inv. no. 12575
184 Photo The Museum of Modern Art, New York/
Scala, Florence. Gift of Philip Johnson. Obj. no.
487.1953
185 Centre Canadien d'Architecture, Montreal.
Ref. no. DR1985:0401
186 Georg Jensen A/S, Copenhagen
187 H. P. Rohde, Copenhagen
188 Pinacoteca Civica di Palazzo Volpi, Como. Inv.
no. A341
189 Pinacoteca Civica di Palazzo Volpi, Como. Inv.
no. A344
190 Fonds Sauvage, SIAF/Cité de l'architecture
et du patrimoine/Archives d'architecture du XXe
siècle. 18 IFA 300/10. Photo Chevojon
191 Photo Aerofilms Ltd
192 Photo courtesy Unilever Merseyside Limited
193 Photo Alfred Hind Robinson/Hulton Archive/
Getty Images
194 Hertfordshire Archives and Local Studies
195 Dr Franz Stoedtner-Archiv
196 Musée des Beaux-Arts de Lyon. Don Madame
Tony Garnier, 1952

Select Bibliography

For a detailed bibliography see Pevsner's *Pioneers of Modern Design*, revised edition, Harmondsworth and Baltimore 1968.

General
H. R. Hitchcock, *Architecture, 19th and 20th Centuries* (Pelican History of Art), Baltimore 1963, revised edition, Harmondsworth 1968.

Countries
France: L. Hautecoeur, *Histoire de l'Architecture classique en France*, vol. VII 1848–1900, Paris 1957.
USA: C. W. Condit, *American Building Art. The Nineteenth Century*, New York 1960.

Movements and Styles
Art Nouveau: S. Tschudi Madsen, *Sources of Art Nouveau*, New York and Oslo 1956.
M. Constantine (ed.) and P. Selz, *Art Nouveau*, New York 1959.
R. Schmutzler, *Art Nouveau*, London 1962 and New York 1964.
H. Seling and others, *Jugendstil*, Heidelberg and Munich 1959.
Concrete: P. Collins, *Concrete*, London 1959.
The Chicago School: C. W. Condit, *Chicago School of Architecture*, Chicago 1964.
Historic American Buildings Survey, *Chicago and Nearby Illinois Area*, ed. J. W. Rudd, Illinois 1966.

Biographical
Garnier: C. Pawlowski, *Tony Garnier*, Paris 1967.
Gaudí: G. R. Collins, *Antonio Gaudí*, New York 1960.
Hoffmann: G. Veronesi, *Josef Hoffmann*, Milan 1956.

Klimt: F. Novotny and J. Dobai, *Gustav Klimt*, London and New York 1968.
Loos: L. Münz, G. Künstler and N. Pevsner, *Adolf Loos*, London and New York 1966.
Mackintosh: T. Howarth, *Charles Rennie Mackintosh and the Modern Movement*, London 1952.
Morris: J. W. Mackail, *The Life of William Morris*, London 1899 (World's Classics edition 1950).
P. Thompson, *The Work of William Morris*, New York 1966 and London 1967.
P. Henderson, *William Morris*, London and New York 1967.
Perret: E. N. Rogers, *Auguste Perret*, Milan 1955.
Shaw: R. Blomfield, *Richard Norman Shaw, R.A.*, London 1940.
Sullivan: H. Morrison, *Louis Sullivan, Prophet of Modern Architecture*, Magnolia, Mass. 1958.
Tiffany: R. Koch, *Louis C. Tiffany, Rebel in Glass*, New York 1964.
Voysey: J. Brandon-Jones, in *Architectural Assn. Jour.*, LXXII, 1957.
Webb: W. R. Lethaby, *Philip Webb and his Works*, Oxford 1935.
Wright: H. R. Hitchcock, *In the Nature of Materials*, New York 1942.

Index

Page numbers in italic refer to illustrations

A
architecture 11–22, 29–62, 90–99, 106–15, 119–26, 134–9, 142–6, 149–70, 173–87, 188–201
Ashbee, C. R. 130, 143, 145–6; *122*

B
Baker, Sir Benjamin *144*
Barlow, William H. *7*
Baudot, Anatole de *145–6*
Beardsley, Aubrey 117, 145
Behrens, Peter 72, 149, 164, 173–7, 179, 180, 199, 201; *174, 175*
Berg, Max 201; *157–8*
Berlage, H. P. 123, 180; *118*
Bernard, Emile 58–61, 68; *46*
Bindesbøll, Thorvald 58–61, 201; *48, 49*
Blake, William 45
book-bindings 49; *62, 63*
Boussiron, Simon 162–4; *155*
Bunning, J. B. 17; *5*
Burne-Jones, Edward 19

C
ceramics and glass 53–7, 58–62, 78, 149
Charpentier, Alexander 84; *76*
Coignet, François 152
Cole, Henry 12, 23, 26, 74

Contamin, V. 17; *8*
Cranach, Wilhelm Lucas von *66*

D
Darby, Abraham *3*
Daum brothers 78; *72, 74*
Donaldson, T. L. 172
D'Aronco, Raimondo 188
Dutert, Ferdinand 19; *8*

E
Eckmann, Otto 84–86; *61*
Eiffel, Gustave 149; *142, 143*
Endell, August 105; *87, 89*

F
Finley, James 14
Fowler, John 149–51; *144*
furniture 23–5, 82–90, 117–19, 149, 187; *10, 73, 74, 75, 77, 78, 79, 80, 81, 82, 110, 111, 122, 134–7, 173, 183, 184*

G
Gaillard, Eugène 84–86
Gallé, Emile 53, 74–5, 78; *37, 39, 75*
Garnier, Tony 160–1, 164, 177, 187, 188, 196; *151, 154, 196*
Gaudí, Antoni 7, 62–68, 88–93, 106, 109, 113–5, 134, 201; *52, 102, 103, 104, 105–109*
Gauguin, Paul 53, 68, 72, 200, 201; *40–5*
Gilbert, Alfred 68, 99–100; *50–51*
Gimson, Ernest 129; *120*
Gropius, Walter 6, 7, 8, 177, 179, 187, 199, 201; *176*
Guimard, Hector 7, 99–100, 106, 156, 167; *96–101*

H
Hennebique, François 106, 152; *147*
Hoentschel, Georges 78; *68*
Hoffmann, Josef 164, 167–8, 170, 179, 201; *140, 162–3, 166*
Hogarth, William 11
Holabird, William 41; *25*
Horta, Victor 7, 45, 67; *87, 90–4*
Howard, Ebenezer 192–4, 196; *194*

J
Jenney, William le Baron 41
Jensen, Georg 188; *186, 187*
jewelry 76–8; *126, 127*
Jones, Owen 12; *14*

J
Klimt, Gustav 168; *163, 166*
Koepping, Karl 78; *72*

L
Labrouste, Henri 17, 152; *6*
Lalique, René *64, 65, 67*
Lemmen, Georges 72; *58*
Lethaby, W. R. 122, 127–9; *120*
Leveillé, E. B. *38*
Lodoli, Abbate 11
Louis, Victor 14
Loos, Adolf 8, 146, 164, 167, 170, 177, 201; *165*
Lutyens, Edwin 122–3, 127; *117*

M
Macdonald sisters, Margaret and Frances 130; *127*
Mackintosh, Charles Rennie 7, 134–46; *126, 129–37*
Mackintosh, Margaret 130; *127*
Mackmurdo, Arthur H. 7, 45–53, 67, 117–9, 129, 130, 145; *28, 29, 33, 34, 110, 111, 112*
Madox Brown, Ford 19–22; *10*
Maillart, Robert 160, 164; *156*
Majorelle, Louis 82; *77*
Marinetti, F. T. 188, 196–9
Martin, Camille *49, 50*
metalwork 64–7, 93–7, 99–105, 188; *94, 95, 96, 97, 123, 124, 126, 127, 168, 186*
Meyer, Adolf 6, 177
Monier, Joseph 152
Morris, William 6, 8, 19–23, 25, 26–30, 34–37, 45–47, 53, 114, 117, 129–30, 145, 192, 200; *11, 12, 13, 29, 73*
Muthesius, Hermann 146, 151, 177, 179

N
Newton, Ernest 117
Nyrop, Martin 123; *119*

O
Obrist, Hermann 55
Olbrich, Joseph 143, 146; *138*

Oud, J. J. P. *185*
Owen, Robert 192

P

Parker, Barry *193*
Paxton, Sir Joseph 2
Perret, Auguste 154, 156, 160,
    164, 167, 179, 201; *148–50*
Prior, E. S. 122, 142; *116*
Pritchard, T. F. *3*
Prouvé, Victor 78; *63, 70, 74*
Pugin, Augustus Welby
    Northmore 11, 12, 15, 18, 26

R

Redgrave, Richard 12
Richardson, H. H. 35–36; *22*
Riemerschmid, Richard 86, 149,
    173; *81, 167, 173, 198*
Rietveld, Gerrit Thomas 187;
    183
Roeblings, the 149
Rohde, Johan *186–7*
Rossetti, Dante Gabriel 19
Rosso, Menardo 188
Rousseau, Eugène *35, 36*
Ruskin, John 15, 22, 46

S

Salt, Sir Titus 192; *191*
Sant'Elia, Antonio 188–92, 199;
    188, 189
Sauvage, Henri 188–92; *190*
Schmidt, Karl 149
Scott, Baillie 129, 140, 142–46;
    193
Scott, Gilbert 18, 19
Sehring, Bernhard 99; *95*
Semper, Gottfried 12
Shaw, Richard Norman 34–37,
    117–20, 122, 130, 192; *15,
    17, 18*
Sommaruga 188
Soufflot 14
Sullivan, Louis 7, 41, 180; *48,
    49, 179*
Sumner, Heywood 49, 58; *32*

T

tapestry and embroidery 58–62
Taut, Bruno 179; *177, 178*
Telford, Thomas *4*
textiles and wallpapers 25–6,
    46–49, 68
Tiffany, Louis C. 78, 115; *71–3*

town planning 160–1, 192–9;
    151
typography and graphic design
    45, 58–62, 72, 145–6

U

Unwin, Sir Raymond 194; *165*

V

Vallin, Eugène 83, 84; *74*
Van de Velde, Henry 6–7, 72–76,
    86, 109, 115, 177, 179; *45, 54,
    59–61, 79*
Viollet-le-Duc, Emanuel 18, 19,
    34–37, 67, 97, 152, 164; *53*
Voysey, C. F. A. 7, 25, 68, 75–6,
    117, 119–20, 122–3, 127, 129,
    130, 134, 142, 145–6, 188; *56,
    57, 113–15, 121, 124*

W

Wagner, Otto *159, 161*
Webb, Philip 6, 19–22, 25–26,
    30–33, 57, 117; *9, 11, 73*
Whistler, James McNeill 45;
    29, 30
White, Stanford *21*
Wiener, René *62, 63*
Wilde, Oscar 172–3
Willumsen, J. F. *47*
Wright, Frank Lloyd 7, 109, 180;
    180–2
Wyatt, Matthew Digby 12, 15, 18

"This kind of book at this kind of price
is what art publishing should be about"
—*New York Times Book Review*

"An extraordinarily rich and varied series"
—Linda Nochlin

The World of Art series is a comprehensive,
accessible, indispensable companion to the history
of art and its latest developments, covering themes,
artists and movements that span centuries and
the gamut of visual culture around the globe.

You may also like:

**American Art and
Architecture**
Michael J. Lewis

Artists' Film
David Curtis
Foreword by Steve McQueen

Bauhaus
Frank Whitford
Introduction by Michael
White

Dada
Hans Richter
Introduction and commentary
by Michael White

Digital Art
Christiane Paul

**Graphic Design in the
Twentieth Century
A Concise History**
Richard Hollis

Interior Design Since 1900
Anne Massey

**Modern Architecture
A Critical History**
Kenneth Frampton

Movements in Art Since 1945
Edward Lucie-Smith

Women in Design
Anne Massey

World of Art

For more information about
Thames & Hudson, and the World of Art
series, visit **thamesandhudsonusa.com**